TRANSFORMED
for a PURPOSE

SAJI LUKOS

Printed in the United States of America

Published by:
Mall Publishing
641 Homewood Avenue
Highland Park, Illinois 60035
1.877.203.2453

Cover Design and Text Design by Marlon B. Villadiego

ISBN #1-934165-36-0
Unless otherwise noted, all scripture quotations are from the New International
Version (NIV) or New King James Version (NKJV) of the Holy Bible.

For licensing / copyright information, for additional copies or for use in
specialized settings contact:

Saji Lukos
RIMI
P.O. Box 688
Round Lake Beach, IL 60073
847-265-0630
slukos@rimi.org
www.rimi.org

TRANSFORMED
for a PURPOSE

SAJI LUKOS

Mall Publishing Co.

THE PRINTED WORD THE PLANTED SEED

HIGHLAND PARK, ILLINOIS

Live in the Light of Eternity
A Challenge from the Heart

Do you think God is dead in the West? Think again! Is your faith lukewarm? Let God relight the fire! Is your church stagnant? Rediscover the passion! Impact eternity! Come invest your life and resources in God's global cause! This book tells you how. The story of Saji Lukos, and of others who share in the vision God gave him, will inspire and challenge you to live in light of eternity. In these pages you will encounter the Living God who is powerfully working in the world today! You will taste how real and personal He is.

In this compelling narrative, Saji shares how God rescued him, and ultimately his entire family, from deep darkness and brought them into His wonderful light. You will come to share Saji's vision for taking Christ to South Asia's lost. Greater still, you will learn how God can use you and your church to change eternal destinies.

After his conversion, God led Saji to establish one of South Asia's leading native missions agencies. Today (2008), RIMI has deployed over 1230 indigenous church planters and established more than 4000 house churches, 26 Bible colleges, and 16 Mercy Homes ministering to more than 600 impoverished children throughout South Asia.

SAJI K. LUKOS

WHAT CHRISTIAN LEADERS ARE SAYING...

Saji Lukos, the visionary of RIMI – Reaching Indians Ministries International - could not be dismissed without listening to what he passionately says about the Gospel for India and beyond. He believes that the Lord has blessed His resources to be released for the kingdom business across the world. With him, his wife and his dedicated team continues to strive to create a vision for the lost with the Gospel. Once you are in touch with him, you cannot be but smitten by the passion and commitment for the Gospel to the ends of the earth beginning from India. Mission India, a ministry of RIMI is a member of India Missions Association.

Dr. K. Rajendran,
General Secretary,
India Missions Association

Saji Lukos has as much claim to the title 'modern apostle to India' than anyone else of whom I am aware. His story is inspiring and humbling and reminds us that one life can make a difference.

Dr. Kevin J. Vanhoozer.
Research Professor of Systematic Theology,
Trinity Evangelical Divinity School

Spending time with Saji in Nagpur, seeing the campus which reminds one of his first glimpse of Jerusalem, engaging with seminary students and faculty, hearing testimonies of miracles and salvation, will refresh any believer's spirit. I look forward to reading the book which I fully expect will be mightily used of God in reaching India for Christ.

Dr. Calvin Hanson
Former President of Trinity Western University,
Vancouver, Canada

The joy of partnering with Saji Lukos and RIMI to "go make disciples" in South Asia has spiritually renewed me and our church. Through our partnership with RIMI, God is using us to impact the world. I am grateful for this book because RIMI's story needs to be told. Even more, RIMI's vision needs to be shared!

Dr. Dean Shriver,
Pastor, Intermountain Baptist Church,
Salt Lake City, Utah

It is impossible to be exposed to Saji Lukos and not be convinced that he is both a man of passion and vision...he exudes them! What has made Saji (and RIMI) successful, however, is that his passion and vision has been channeled into a well-defined strategic plan. This inspiring book highlights Saji's passion and vision...but it also details a careful plan that God has greatly honored!

Rev. Bob Boerner, Jr.,
Director of Young Business Leaders,
Huntsville, Alabama

It is my joy to commend to you Transformed for a Purpose by Rev Saji K. Lukos. The story of what God has done in his life these past twenty-seven years will be an encouragement to all who read it. May our Lord use this story to His own honor and glory to see multitudes of others transformed by the same power of God.

Dr. Walter C.Kaiser,Jr.
President Emeritus,
Colman M. Mockler Distinguished Professor of Old Testament,
Gordon-Conwell Theological Seminary,
Hamilton, MA, USA

I highly recommend this thrilling story of a man transformed by the grace of God, and who is passionate that his fellow Indians are similarly transformed. My fellow Scott, John Knox, cried, *"Give me Scotland or I die!"* Read how the Lord answered and continues to answer Saji's cry from his heart, *"Give me India or I die!"*

Dr. John H. Munro,
Senior Pastor, Calvary Church,
Charlotte, North Carolina

Here is a moving autobiography, a graphic picture of life in India, insights into the way God calls and leads, motivating descriptions of people God has used, principles for the future of world-wide missions--all this plus a love story and colorful observations by Saji's wife Moni and others! It is a remarkable and gripping narrative by a true man of God, Saji Lukos.

Dr. Walter Liefeld,
New Testament Scholar, Retired Professor,
Trinity International University, IL

A story that will both inspire and instruct. By reading this not only will you rejoice at what God is doing in the world today, you will also be challenged and guided about how you too can be involved in God's glorious plan for the world.

Dr. Ajith Fernando,
National Director Youth for Christ, Sri Lanka,
and Bible teacher and author

Transformed for a Purpose is an engaging volume because it unveils the adventurous and energetic life journey of a purpose-driven and passion-filled global missions mobilizer. Saji Lukos extends a compelling invitation to believers to get involved and invest in the spiritual and social transformation of millions in the land of his birth. I am convinced that India is not only propelling to become a global economic powerhouse but it is also being prepared by ministry agencies like RIMI to reap an unprecedented spiritual harvest. Why not adopt a Kingdom of God lifestyle and partner to make an eternal difference.

Rev. Dr. T.V. Thomas,
Co-Chair, International Network of South Asian Diaspora Leaders
(INSADL)

Saji's story will challenge and encourage you to grasp fully God's love for all nations. Jesus commanded us to continue his ministry, and Saji has obeyed that command in the most challenging areas of India. You can't read his story without asking: 'God, what would you have me do?'

Dr. George Davis,
Senior Pastor, Salem Evangelical Free Church,
Fargo, ND

Saji writes with passion from an experience with Christ that overflows through the book. His story will both inspire and challenge the reader to greater resolve to seek first the Kingdom. I commend it to you.

Dr. Robert E. Coleman,
Distinguished Professor of Discipleship and Evangelism,
Gordon Conwell Theological Seminary;
Author of the Master Plan of Evangelism

DEDICATION

This book is dedicated to my family— Moni, my wife, and Maryann, my daughter— and the indigenous laborers of South Asia who serve the Lord with such fervor and faith.

TABLE OF CONTENTS

Acknowledgements..*xv*

Foreword by Robert Schill..*xvii*

Introduction..*xix*

Part I – Moving into the Light

   1. The Dominion of Darkness 3

   2. Fighting for Peace.. 7

   3. Finding the Light 13

   4. Struggling in the Shadows... 17

   5. Following the Father 23

   6. She is Good for You 31

Part II – Moving to the Land of Opportunity

   7. Pursuing God's Call... 43

   8. Life in the Windy City... 47

   9. Give Me India or Let Me Die....................................... 53

   10. America's Kindness and Generosity........................... 57

Part III – Moving Ahead with God's Vision

   11. The Year of Two Births 63

   12. Organizing the Vision.. 81

   13. God's Provision for the Vision 87

Part IV – Moving Out in Action

   14. One Village at a Time 93

15. Training Tomorrow's Leaders.. 103

16. Called to Compassion.. 123

17. Indigenous Ownership 129

18. Stewardship - Our Calling... 135

19. Partnering with the Global Church 141

Part V – Moving Ahead in Partnerships

20. A Hunger for the Truth ~ *Richard P. Carlson*................................ 167

21. India is My Second Home ~ *Laura Grimaldi*................................ 175

22. God is Moving with Power ~ *Thomas P. Dooley*............................ 179

23. Jesus – Above All Other Gods ~ *Linda Kahaanui* 185

24. Numbers from the 10/40 Window ~ *Douglas Stewart*................. 191

25. The Joy of Strategic Investing ~ *Bob Ancha*................................ 199

26. Partnership Opportunities 205

Acknowledgments

A countless number of people have touched my life over the years. Two individuals who have made a deep impact are Pastor John Ninan and Pastor A.V. Thomas who shared Christ with me in spite of my lack of receptivity. Undaunted by the threats from my family, they continued to love and disciple me for which I will always be grateful.

I extend heartfelt thanks to Imogene Glassmeyer who lived in the Denver area and was like a mother to me. There were numerous times when she picked me up from the airport and handed over her car keys so I could travel in and around Denver. Her house was a home away from home. Over the years she encouraged me to write a book about my life and the vision of Reaching Indians Ministries International (RIMI). Before her death, she visited South Asia twice and blessed us by giving financially towards the down payment of our home and the temporary RIMI office in Round Lake Beach, Illinois.

I am grateful to Rachel Holmes, Ilene Foote, Dean Shriver, Philip Hess, and others who offered suggestions and helped edit this book. Special thanks also to the staff teams of RIMI and Mission India (MI), especially Steve Ernst and Ernest Mall, for their help and management of this book's production.

I am also grateful to those who have contributed to this book by sharing their experiences and the relevance of indigenous missions today- Robert Schill, Thomas Dooley, Robert Ancha, Linda Kaahanui, Laura Grimaldi, Rich Carlson, Doug Steward, and a host of Christian leaders and other friends who have encouraged me with their endorsements.

My greatest debt goes to the two special ladies in my life: my wife,

Moni, and my daughter, Maryann. Their emotional and spiritual support have allowed me time and focus to write amidst the numerous challenges of the ministry. I travel many miles every year and am away from them constantly for the sake of Jesus. Moni and Maryann, thank you for your love, continued prayers, and support.

FOREWORD
BY
ROBERT SCHILL, RIMI BOARD CHAIRMAN

A Remarkable Man

It was the fall of 2000. Bombay was just reverting to its Indian name of Mumbi. The airport there was very hot and crowded. My wife, Jan, and I had come to India to help develop a plan for a new seminary in Nagpur, the geographic center of India. As we emerged from the airport, we saw and met Saji Lukos for the first time. He introduced himself and India to us. From that first meeting until now, our relationship has blessed me and my service to Christ.

In response to God's increasing call, I had recently retired from my large architectural practice of 35 years to serve Him more directly in the work of missions. Now in India, working closely with Saji, I began a ministry of "helps" to RIMI in developing the physical Master Site Plan and facilities for the Mission India Theological Seminary (MITS). Over the years my service has expanded to design other RIMI ministry facilities, both in India and the United States. Through working closely with Saji, being with him and his family, and traveling extensively with him, I have come to see him as one who has been called to God's work – a remarkable man of God.

I have seen in Saji his clear call by God to be a Christ-like leader in missions. His love for our Lord is unflagging; his walk with Christ "fresh"; and his devotion to reaching Indians throughout the world zealously passionate. God, through Saji, is making a significant impact on India. He maximizes God's resources through RIMI and has an infectious enthusiasm for Christ and RIMI. He looks strategically to the future, providing visionary leadership to all facets of the RIMI and Mission India ministry. His seemingly inexhaustible energy and travels for the work continues to forge ever increasing strategic partnerships to strengthen and expand God's outreach to South Asians.

Saji is important to my life. His life is an outstanding, ongoing example of God's power and grace worked through a yielded life.

"Give me India or let me die," the prayer Saji prayed, is not just a slogan for Saji—it is the ongoing passion of his life! I am thankful and grateful to God for him.

INTRODUCTION

In 1979, at age twenty, God brought me out of darkness and into His wonderful light. It was the first time in my life that I enjoyed lasting peace. However, because of my new found faith, I was persecuted and disowned by my family. Yet, in spite of their ignorance and hatred, I prayed passionately for their salvation. God answered! Within eight years, every member of my family received Christ and was radically transformed. Today, they possess the same joy and sense of purpose God first gave me.

As I grew in my Christian faith, my passion for God increased along with an intense burden for people. I brought many people to Christ while running a business school in India. In 1986, I married a beautiful Indian girl, Moni, who grew up in New York. Soon after, I immigrated to New York to pursue "the American dream." While I was working in New York, God clearly spoke to me through 1 John 2:15-17. For six months I meditated on the truth, ...*but the man who does the will of God lives forever.* I knew God was preparing and challenging me to seek His will instead of my own life's ambition and agenda.

Through prayer, and the experiences and trials described in this book, God led and enabled me to establish two ministries—Reaching Indians Ministries International (RIMI) in North America and Mission India (MI) in India. Both ministries focus on reaching South Asians worldwide by establishing churches, developing leaders, and showing the compassion of God through various humanitarian projects.

The One who called us to this work is faithful. The vision God brought to life in 1993 has born, and continues to bear, the fruit of miracles. Today, RIMI has over 1200 field staff, 26 Bible training centers and a major seminary (Mission India Theological Seminary) in Nagpur, central India. We also have 16 Mercy Homes caring for the welfare of more than 600 children—and growing fast. These tangible fruits are the result of answered prayer and intentional giving by believers.

Today, God continues to raise up indigenous leaders across South Asia. He is graciously building on the sacrificial work of Western missionaries who, in the past, poured their lives out for Christ in foreign lands. Presently, however, many Asian nations are restricting access to Western missionaries. The new challenge for the Western Church is to come alongside nationals (i.e. Christian workers serving in their countries of origin) with a spirit of humility and cooperation so that indigenous leadership can be fully developed, resulting in a mature and growing national Church. The Western Church can accomplish this by strategically supporting church plants and capital projects in their beginning stages. Such partnerships result in healthy "jump-starts" for infant local churches enabling them to become financially independent and spiritually mature.

Supporting national workers with prayer and finances is fruitful! In a brief span of time, national workers are bringing unbelievers to Christ at an exponential rate. One of our church-planters baptized forty-two new believers after serving in one village for only five months. When the obstacles faced by an expatriate missionary are considered (cross-cultural preparation, learning a new language, adapting to a new culture, support raising for living and ministry expenses, etc.), it becomes clear that national workers typically face far fewer difficulties establishing themselves on the field. Today, God is multiplying the number of humble, dedicated national workers taking Christ to the nations. In light of global changes, the strategy of Western believers partnering alongside their South Asian brothers and sisters is not only biblical, but God-honoring, and highly productive.

This type of partnership makes sense. Partnering together benefits every part of the Body of Christ. The West has God-given resources and national workers need support. Together, we can partner to change the lives and destinies of millions of unreached people. This happens when we bring our attitudes and lifestyles in line with God's priorities. Let us, however, be aware of Satan's schemes. He seeks to divide us. Scripture clearly teaches us that Jesus is the only way to salvation (John 14:6; Acts 4:12). We must act on this truth by submitting to Him and uniting together as one Body so we can complete the unfinished task of world evangelism before Christ returns.

I trust this book will challenge and convict you. My life's journey and the journeys of others recorded here, manifest God's power to change destinies. God transforms our lives for a purpose—to impact the world for His glory. It is my desire, as you read this book, that you will be eager to experience the presence of the living God in your personal life and then you will get involved passionately in world missions. I pray these stories of national missionaries—and the Western believers who partner with them—will stir your passion to join in what God is doing in South Asia and beyond! As we partner together to fulfill the Great Commission, my dream is that God will raise up 100,000 Christ-like, global leaders to reach South Asia and the world during my lifetime. So friends, will you dream with me?

I'm always reminded by the words of Christ in Matthew 5:8, "Blessed are the pure in heart, for they will see God." It is my commitment to my God and everyone to live with integrity of heart and finish well the task He has entrusted to me.

Saji K. Lukos

February 28, 2007

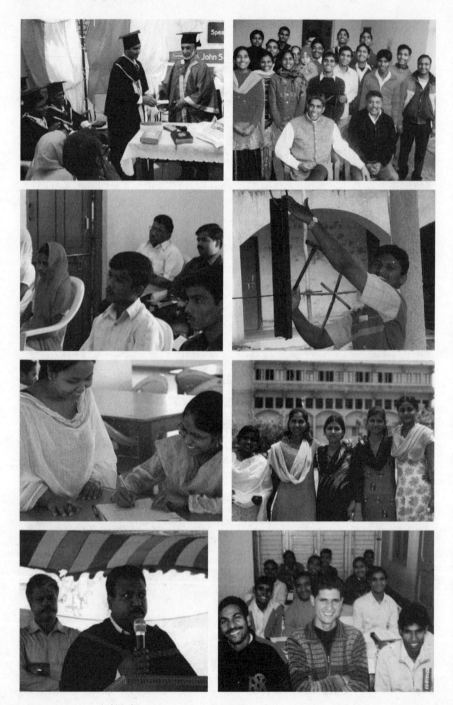

PART I
MOVING INTO THE LIGHT
The Testimony and Calling of Saji Lukos

1

THE DOMINION OF DARKNESS

*The enemy pursues me, he crushes me to the ground; he makes
me dwell in darkness like those long dead. So my spirit grows
faint within me; my heart within me is dismayed.*

~ *Psalm 143:3-4*

Vengoor Village, Kerala, South India, 1972 . . . at 3:00 a.m. in
the morning my father realized that my mother was not in bed.
He called me and we took candles to light our search. I was around
thirteen, the oldest of eight children. Looking for my mother, I called
out to her loudly, "Amma!" as we walked around our property.

About fifty feet from the
house, I found her under a
cashew tree, blood flowing from
the wound on her neck. She had
cut herself with a knife from
the kitchen. I remember being

> **Looking for my mother,
> I called out to her loudly,
> "Amma!" as we walked
> around our property.**

afraid and crying as my father took my mother back into the house.

He sent my uncle, who ran four miles, to find a taxi in a city of
millions. At that time cars were scarce. He managed to grab a taxi and
my father took my mother to the hospital. After a week of treatments,

she was discharged and returned home. She later related to us that during her hospital stay she often heard a voice commanding her to take her own life by committing various acts—such as climbing trees and throwing herself from them. The evil spirit had been tormenting her and others in my family for many years.

Our family was religious and nominally Christian, but we did not know the truth. We deliberately rejected God and His commands. We were blind to Satan's schemes and too weak to defend ourselves against his attacks by which he took hold of our home and family.

Satan tormented us in many ways. My mother heard his taunting voice. My sister was demon-possessed. My father was proud, bitter, and an alcoholic. I was hopeless and festered with anger—abhorring anyone or anything opposing me. Earlier in the week of my mother's attempted suicide, I smashed her cooking pots in a raging tantrum because, without my permission, she sold the cashews I picked so she could buy supplies for the family. Darkness pervaded our lives. However, even as Satan and his demons tightened their chains around our family, God faithfully preserved us for His own purpose. When my father was bitten by a Cobra, he miraculously recovered, after only one week in the hospital! We didn't know it, but during those terrible years God's hand of protection was on us.

Through prayer and faith in God's promises we can obstruct his deadly plans.

Just like Satan worked to thwart God's gracious plan for my family, he continues to work today. Satan's tactics have not changed. He still uses lies, deception, murder, and a host of other destructive tactics to accomplish his evil purposes. As believers, we must familiarize ourselves with his schemes. Through prayer and faith in God's promises we can obstruct his deadly plans. In the same way Satan tempted Eve to sin against God in the Garden of Eden, he tempted Jesus in the desert. His greatest goal was to cause Jesus to fail in His mission as Messiah. However, Satan failed miserably! In His death and resurrection, Jesus conquered Satan once for all. Today we can share His victory and experience it in our own lives. Satan uses temptation, doubt, guilt, fear, confusion, division, sickness, envy, pride, slander, and any other means possible to hinder God's work in our lives. This is just as true in the West as it is in the East. We see Satan at work in divided churches, divorces, abortions, drug use, violence, alcoholism, gambling, and other addictive pleasure-seeking pursuits. Satan is the "father of lies" (John 8:44). He works to destroy our personal lives, our families, and our societies by blinding us to the authority of God and His Word.

Thankfully, God has limited Satan's power. As the biblical story of Job tells us, Satan can only do what God gives him permission to do and nothing more (Job 1:12; 2:6). Demons are kept in "eternal chains" (Jude 6) and can be resisted by Christians through the power and authority that Christ gives us (James 4:7). Satan's influence consists only of what God allows.

Today, Satan suppresses and tortures all of South Asia, attempting to keep the land bound in darkness. But the One who is in us is greater than the one who is in the world (1 John 4:4)! The time has come for Satan's chains to be removed. What an exciting time it is! God is moving in people's hearts, bringing them from darkness into His light. Today I am privileged beyond measure to be a servant of God's redeeming work in South Asia. However, before God enlisted me in His work, He had to bring light into my dark soul and turn me from my life of sin.

2

Fighting for Peace

Other sins find their vent in the accomplishment of evil deeds,
whereas pride lies in wait for good deeds, to destroy them.

~ St. Augustine

Kerala, the beautiful State in India where I grew up, means "Land of Coconuts." Proudly called "God's own country," Kerala is located in the southern tip of India and is an evergreen state—home to beaches, mountains, inland waterways, and jungles. There are various religions, communism, matrilineal social structures, spice trade, and a long history of rule by kings called "maharajahs."

The history of Kerala is as lush as the vegetation indigenous to the area. Christianity is believed to have arrived in Kerala in AD 52 with the coming of Saint Thomas, known as "Doubting Thomas". This apostle of Christ spread the Gospel message in the state and beyond. Oral history has passed down a story still told today. When St. Thomas arrived on the shores of India, he asked the locals a question, "If I threw water up in the air and it did not come down, would you believe in my God?" They answered that they would. When he tossed the water up into the air, it did not come back down and the people believed. Also, according to oral and recorded history of that time period, St. Thomas planted many early churches in South India before he was martyred.

Christianity has made its mark in Kerala's educational, business, and health systems. Kerala stands in the forefront of Indian states in literacy and education. According to the 2001 census, the literacy rate in Kerala is 90%, which is double that of some states in India. Kerala's education of women and its literacy rate compares with the

Christianity is believed to have arrived in Kerala in AD 52 with the coming of Saint Thomas, known as "Doubting Thomas".

most advanced countries of the world. It almost goes without saying that Kerala's history of Christian and educational influences touched my life. In other words, my siblings and I all attended school.

We lived on a farm about two miles away from the middle school. We didn't own a clock. I watched the sun's shadow on the ground as I performed my chores, hurrying so that I could leave for school. Chores, such as taking care of the chickens and other animals, had to be completed before I could go off to school each morning—not an easy feat for a little boy! I often ended up running barefoot through the rice fields, hoping to get to school on time. After school, I helped my family by working in the fields and selling our farm produce in the village market.

As was the custom for the firstborn, my birth was in my mother's village, near Thiruvella, which was about forty miles from my father's village. Following tradition, my mother temporarily moved to her village two months before I was born to receive care from the women in her family who prepared her for motherhood. With the help of a midwife, I was born in my uncle's house. My aunts and other relatives took care of me while my mother regained her strength. She was given massages and cosmetic care, and rested while relatives tended to me. After a few months, my mother and I went back home to live with my father.

My mother's parents were no longer living and the only grandparent I knew while growing up was my paternal grandfather. His wife died when my father was six years old. Grandpa never remarried, but single-handedly raised my father and his four siblings. They grew up discouraged and helpless without the love of their mother. My father did not get a chance to pursue educational studies beyond eighth grade because of his responsibilities on the family farm. The household responsibilities fell to my father's oldest sister.

We only became close years later when I was changed by Jesus and was privileged to lead him to Christ.

Grandpa was strong, stubborn, serious, and full of anger. I was afraid of him during my growing-up years. We only became close, years later, when I was changed by Jesus and was privileged to lead him to Christ. I remember hearing Grandpa tell many stories of my father's rebellious youth. I believe the memories of my father's own rebellious past impacted his decisions in our upbringing, resulting in his strict rule over us. We were never allowed to visit neighbors, play with the village boys, or eat any food from the roadside vendors. Most of the time, my siblings and I simply lived in the closed walls of our family farm.

I always felt a spiritual thirst but did not know how to find the truth. I did not understand the sermons of the priest who came to our village church monthly to perform mass. My mother was a religious and pious woman who often got up early in the morning, placed a mat on the floor, and led us in prayers. My father rarely joined us. There were times when she gave money to local pastors who visited our house and to others in need. This caused tension between my parents because she took money from my father without asking. Regardless of her ritualistic practices, she did not understand the whole teaching of the Bible. Her practices were performed out of love for people and the God she did not yet know.

Our house had only two rooms and a small kitchen. It was too small for my family of nine, but my parents could not afford a bigger house. We all slept on the floor in the same two rooms. There were no shelves or closets in the rooms, so we hung our clothes on a string across the walls. There was no electricity and I remember on one dark evening studying for hours using a kerosene lamp. The next day we were all dismayed—our newly washed clothes were discolored from the kerosene smoke.

My father had good intentions. He tirelessly worked to take care of us and give us a prosperous future. We were grateful for his provision, yet I grew up afraid of him because of his anger and quick temper. His pride and spiritual ignorance caused many problems during my childhood. I once fought with a student at school. My father got involved and beat the boy. As a result, the entire village turned against us. When I was around ten years old, the bishop of our denomination came to our village for a special occasion involving a family in our church. As the family posed with the bishop for a picture, I wanted to have my picture taken with him too. I joined the group. My dad motioned for me to come out of the group. I ignored him, shaming him in public. To make matters worse, he quarreled with the family getting the picture taken. By the end of the event, he was furious. He brutally beat me to the point that I collapsed. I quickly grew to respect my dad, but not out of love—out of fear. I often asked my mother in desperation, "When will we ever have peace in this home?"

After eighth grade, I went to live with my uncle so I could receive a better education. He lived in our state's capitol city, about fifty miles from home. To put it bluntly, it was a living hell. After school, I was forced to work in my uncle's soda factory. My uncle was an alcoholic full of anger who verbally abused his children and me. We lived like mice before a cat.

I was allowed to attend my uncle's church only. The Gospel was not taught there. However, at school I heard exciting, godly words from a committed Christian teacher who loved me and prayed for me. During this time, personal inner struggles and hopelessness often brought thoughts of ending my own life. Providentially, I never attempted to kill myself. One weak moment would have taken my life away— but the Lord protected me from death for the sake of His eternal

We lived like mice before a cat.

plan. I prayed many times for direction and God's deliverance from my situation. I did not know then what it meant to surrender my life to Christ. I did not understand the words of Christ in Matthew 11:28-30, *"Come to me, all you who labor and are heavy laden, and I will give you rest. Take my yoke upon you and learn from me, for I am gentle and lowly in heart, and you will find rest for your souls. For my yoke is easy and my burden is light."*

3

FINDING THE LIGHT

"Men occasionally stumble over the truth, but most of them
pick themselves up and hurry off as if nothing ever happened."
~ *Sir Winston Churchill*

In 1979, I was in the second year of my bachelor's degree in business studying at a Catholic college. Because of the noise and upheaval in our small, crowded home, I asked my father if I could stay in a nearby lodge for a few months in order to better focus on my studies. The lodge was located five miles from our house and ten miles from the college. He gave me permission to go as ordained by God.

As a good student, I was also involved in sports and college politics. Politics gave me the sense of purpose in life that was missing. But it was superficial. My involvement in the student union often led to fighting with opposition parties and participating in destructive pursuits. I later regretted all the acts I committed in order to please other team members and to prove my abilities and strength. It was in those tumultuous days I discovered that God had gifted me in the art of public speaking. Speaking in front of people and arguing points of view did not intimidate me—though at the time, my opinions were not in line with Scripture.

While I was living in the lodge, two young evangelists, John Ninan and A.V. Thomas, visited me. They came at the suggestion of an old woman who was distantly related to my family. She was staying near the lodge in a house owned by her son. John and A.V. had recently graduated from a Bible college in Kerala, now called Faith Theological Seminary. John, a talented singer, was given the gift of teaching God's Word effectively to large groups of people. A.V. Thomas was given the gift of fervent in evangelism and preaching. They used their gifts to minister in the two villages assigned to them. They had little financial support. They received the equivalent of five dollars monthly to pay rent. They trusted God to meet their needs. They walked many miles every day, visited homes, and shared the message of Christ in the mornings. In the evenings, they conducted open air meetings for large crowds. As people heard God's Word they confessed their sins and accepted Christ. The book of Acts came to life right where I lived!

> **They explained John 3:16, "For God so loved the world that he gave his one and only son, that whosoever believes in him should not perish, but have everlasting life."**

One evening as I studied for my second year final examination, John and A.V. arrived at my room and lovingly shared the Gospel. It was the first time in my life that the Gospel was clearly conveyed to me. They explained John 3:16, *"For God so loved the world that he gave his one and only son, that whosoever believes in him should not perish, but have eternal life."* They showed me other passages regarding salvation, but I was proud and arrogant. I rejected their message. After praying for me, they left.

Still, God was graciously preparing my heart to obey Him. Even though I rejected the message and the messengers, they came back a second evening and shared the Gospel with me once again. Because of sin and pride, I hatefully responded, "Please do not disturb my studies." Though there was no joy or peace in my life, I was not willing to surrender due to allegiance to family traditions and fear of my father. I also thought that "born again Christianity" was for poor people, untouchable Dalits and for people of other cultures.

My burden was removed and in the midst of life's uncertainties a new hope welled up within me.

My family, rooted in Syrian Orthodox Christianity, boasted in church tradition and respect for its clergy more than in Christ.

The two men continued to visit me for the next five days, confronting me with the truth that I was a sinner who needed Christ. John challenged me, "Saji, you are a sinner. Now reason with Christ." Yet, I continued to reject them and their message. However, God in His unwavering faithfulness was strongly moving in my spirit. He made me restless. I wanted the joy and new life the evangelists conveyed by sharing Scriptures like 2 Corinthians 5:17, *"Therefore if anyone is in Christ, he is a new creation; old things have passed away; behold, all things have become new."* I wanted to experience the peace John 16:33 speaks of, *"These things have I spoken to you, that in me you may have peace. In the world you will have tribulation; but be of good cheer, I have overcome the world."* I felt the weight of the sin and guilt described in Romans 3:23 *"For all have sinned and fall short of the glory of God."* Like the Prodigal Son of Luke 15:11-32, I was moving towards renewal. Despite my father's strict rule and the bondage of family traditions, I was growing hungry to follow Christ.

As these two men continued to share God's Word with me, I

15

pondered the life-changing truth they introduced me to. Seeds of joy and peace began to take root in me. When John and A.V. came again on the sixth day, April 30, 1979, I prayed and surrendered my life to Christ. There was no defense. I knelt down in tears. As I prayed and confessed my life of sin, I fully yielded my heart to Jesus. These men laid their hands on me, prayed for my spiritual birth into the family of God, and asked Him to bless me. My spirit was instantly and irrevocably refreshed and relieved. My burden was removed and, in the midst of life's uncertainties, a new hope welled up within me. I was immeasurably happy—but also afraid of my father. I knew he would be very angry with me because of my newfound faith.

4

STRUGGLING IN THE SHADOWS

This is my command: Love each other. If the world hates
you, keep in mind that it hated me first. If you belonged to the
world, it would love you as its own. As it is, you do not belong
to the world, but I have chosen you out of the world.
That is why the world hates you.

~ John 15:17-19

Fear of persecution was partly to blame for my initial resistance to the Gospel. When I first heard the Gospel from John Ninan and A.V. Thomas, I thought of my great aunt. My family disowned her when she became a born again Christian. She and I had never met because her brothers warned her not to come around us. That knowledge deeply impacted me. By the grace of God, I was able to overcome my hesitation.

Shortly after God saved me, Pastor T. G. Koshy, the founder of Faith Theological Seminary, baptized me. By this act, I publicly declared that I now belonged to Christ and that I would follow Him as long as I lived.

While I knew I would suffer persecution, nothing could have prepared me for the day my father showed up at the lodge. I had not yet told my family about my conversion. Even so, word spread quickly and found its way back home. My father soon appeared at my door brandishing a knife.

That day is still vivid in my mind. When my father showed up with a knife in hand, my heart began to race and pound in my chest. Between answering and pleading with him not to do anything rash, my heart cried out to Jesus for the strength and peace that only comes from Him.

"Where are your pastors?" he asked me, waving the knife around.

"They are not here," I answered, praying even more fervently.

"I will kill you for bringing shame to my family." The words not only sent chills down my spine, but pierced my heart. "I ought to kill you! You are coming home with me right now. You will see what happens to a son who shames his family."

Panic set in. "What about my exams? I am ready to graduate!" I said, eyeing the knife he was waving in front of me.

"I don't care about that! You *are* coming home!"

With that he pushed me, kicked me, and dragged me home. I could not resist him. He was my father and I wanted to respect him. Beyond this, his violence demanded obedience. No explanations! No pleading for him to understand! And definitely no sharing of my new faith in the living Christ!

Once we arrived home, my father tore strips of fiber hanging from a pepper tree and began to beat me with them over and over again. He beat me as a punishment and a warning to my brothers, sisters, and mother. No member of his family was going to become a Christian and escape his punishment. In his eyes, my faith brought shame on the family. Even as my mother cried, "Stop, you're going to kill him!" he beat me harder, exclaiming, "I do not care! He deserves to die for what he did!"

Then, just as suddenly as my father appeared at the door of my room at the lodge, my parents turned on each other. My father blamed my mother for my "shameful" decision to follow Jesus. "See what you've done!" he wailed. This cut me as deeply as the strips of fiber cut my skin. In his hardness of heart, my father momentarily turned his attention away from me and began beating her.

The neighbors had gathered and, from a distance, watched my father rage against me and my faith. When he became aware of the crowd and its morbid fascination, he yanked me to my feet and pushed me towards a room in our house.

Once there, he bound my feet and hands and left me. The door closed and darkness blanketed me. Even so, by God's grace, the door of my heart stayed open and the light of Christ filled it. I clung to my faith and called on my Lord to give me peace and strength.

My mother soon came in. She gave me water and began to wash my wounds. She asked me how I could turn my back on the family, disgrace them, and abandon them. She questioned how I could become a believer in view of the educational opportunities they had given me. "Your father has worked hard to send you to school," she said, "and this is how you repay him?"

I wanted to weep because of her lack of understanding. Following God did not mean I was abandoning them. "I haven't deserted my family," I explained. "I have found an eternal peace."

Suddenly my father's figure darkened the doorway and my mother stood up, moving away from my side. He hovered over me. "You are no longer my son. Get out of my home!"

I straightened my shoulders and looked in his eyes before calmly saying, "Go ahead and kill me. I will not back down from my faith."

"Get out!"

I gathered my few belongings, some books and a briefcase, took one last look at my family and walked out. All I had ever known in my home was much sorrow and pain. I grieved over the brokenness that marked the lives of my siblings and parents. I left that day knowing that this might be the last time I would ever see any of them again.

I returned to the lodge. My Christian friends comforted me with their prayers and friendship. They opened their hearts to me and helped supply my financial needs. They stood by my side during that difficult time, loving and supporting me.

I told John Ninan that God had spoken words of comfort to my heart from Psalms 27:10, *"Though my father and mother forsake me, the LORD will receive me."* John also pointed out reassuring words in Hebrews 13:5-6, *"...God has said 'Never will I leave you; never will I forsake you.' So we say with confidence, 'The Lord is my helper; I will not be afraid. What can man do to me?'"*

During the previous few days, my earthly father had beaten and rejected me. The only home I had ever known was lost to me. Still, I found strength and hope in Jesus. I prayed that my heavenly Father would honor my steadfastness by helping me reach my earthly father one day. That day would be long in coming.

> **"Though my father and mother forsake me, the LORD will receive me."**

Over the next several months, I shared my testimony in churches to encourage others who had suffered similar trials. I finished my final exams and graduated with a Bachelor in Business degree. Shortly thereafter, I moved to Thiruvananthapuram, the capital of Kerala, to study for a Masters in Business and Cost Accounting. I turned the page to a new chapter in my life. Even though my heart was burdened for my family and others living in spiritual darkness—I packed my belongings, clung to my new-found faith, and moved from the shadows into the light.

5

FOLLOWING THE FATHER

*Character cannot be developed in ease and quiet. Only through
experience of trial and suffering can the soul be strengthened,
vision cleared, ambition inspired, and success achieved.*

~ *Helen Keller*

I arrived in Thiruvananthapuram in 1980, and began to pursue a
Masters Degree in Business and Cost Accounting. I rented a lodge
room in the neighborhood of Palayam. Palayam is home to three
religious worship centers. There is the historic Catholic Church and
a cross from it is the mosque and adjacent to the mosque is a Hindu
temple. The owner of the lodge, Mr. Johnson, was gracious and
rented me a room at a low price. My roommate was a Muslim named
Salim, who was studying for his Master of Arts degree. We became
good friends and I often shared Christ with him. He prayed with me
but never fully accepted Christ as his Savior and Lord. We remained
friends for more than twenty years. Sadly, I found out that he recently
died of a heart attack while working in the Middle East. As far as I
know, he never accepted Christ as his personal Savior. It is sobering to
think of friends who face eternity without Christ!

While studying in Palayam, I rose early in the mornings and—after
a time of prayer and personal devotions—tutored students in their

homes before they left for school. Tutoring provided me with about fifteen dollars a month. This modest income paid for my studies,

In Indian culture, the oldest son is like a second father in the home.

food, and accommodations. I often ate only one meal a day in order to make ends meet. Tutoring provided me with the opportunity to meet many parents and develop networks with distinguished people in the city. After I finished tutoring each morning, I went to the university library and prepared for my business classes. In the evenings, I worked on a second degree at the Institute of Cost Accounting.

Through a connection with a Christian bank manager from my village, I found a thriving church in the center of Thiruvananthapuram. The church was loving, caring, and attracted many young people. Full of evangelistic enthusiasm, they reached out to the college students. God blessed their ministry and many unsaved and nominal Christian students became avid followers of Christ. It was a thrill to be part of this church family!

I continued to be burdened for my parents and siblings back home. I cried out to God every evening for their salvation. I prayed, "Lord, I'm happy, but I will not be fully satisfied until you bring every member of my family into the enjoyment of your riches."

In Indian culture, the oldest son is like a second father in the home. He is responsible for taking care of his younger siblings by providing jobs and finding spouses for them. God compelled me to fulfill my responsibility as the oldest son in my family. I brought my brother Regi to join me in the city so he could pursue his own studies. He worked part-time with an architect. This provided him with an income and also prepared him for his future business and ministry. As Regi grew to know and accept Jesus, we began to pray together for our family. One day, God prompted me to rent a house so I could bring more of my siblings to the city and help them improve their lives spiritually, educationally, and economically. However, there was a problem with this plan—I didn't have enough money. God led me to borrow money from a brother in Christ from my church. He was kind and gave me the exact amount of money I asked for. I rented a two room house from a Hindu family.

During this time, God opened the door for me to teach business courses at a local private college. There I prayed for each of my students and earned the respect of my colleagues even though most of them were not Christians. God's ways are beyond comprehension. Although I did not understand it at the time, He was preparing me for my future ministry. In the university classroom, I discovered that God had given me the gift of teaching. Today, this is my strongest spiritual gift. It fulfills me to see God change lives through the teaching of His Word.

In 1983, I graduated with a Masters in Business and Cost Accounting and God began to open new doors. With my degree and teaching experience, I founded a private business school called Commerce Study Center. In India, students can earn their degree at either a government recognized school or a non-recognized private school. The only requirement is they pass the university's comprehensive exam. Beginning with a class of six, I tutored university students and coached others preparing for their comprehensive exams. I loved and cared about my students. As more students came to study at the center, I hired some part-time teachers to help. Eventually, we found ourselves tutoring between 100-200 students each year.

Commerce Study Center provided the income I needed to support

—
25

my family and support missions. By this time a few more of my siblings had joined Regi and me in the city. These included two sisters, Lissy and Jessy, and a brother, Matthew. Lissy took on the role of a mother and managed the household. She became the spiritual fire in the family, praying and fasting regularly.

It is remarkable to think about the way God was transforming us into a Christian family in the city. Before we knew Christ, our years in the village were marked by oppression and fragmentation. For generations, my family had been victimized by Satan but now, he was losing ground. After years of being victimized by Satan, Lissy found victory in Christ. Lissy's childhood was fraught with Satanic oppression. He manifested himself in her by talking through her in the voice of my grandmother who had died forty years earlier. The demon, masquerading as my grandmother, threatened my grandfather and father. She demanded a better grave stone. If they refused to provide it, one of my siblings would die. Full of fear, my grandfather and father sought relief from magicians. They also traveled several hours to attend a church festival where they sacrificed chickens in an attempt to pacify the demon who spoke through Lissy.

Once I became a Christian and began to pray and bring the Gospel to my family, Satan's demonic vengeance intensified. God powerfully responded with miracles of deliverance. When Lissy was thirteen, Satan attacked her at school. She became demon possessed. A school boy rushed to our home where A.V. Thomas was visiting me. We ran through the rice field to the school and found Lissy lying on a table with many students and teachers surrounding her. A.V. Thomas asked for a glass of water. He prayed over it and sprinkled the water over my sister's face while rebuking the demon in the name of Jesus to leave her body. Immediately Lissy woke up—surprised to find me at the school. Never again did Satan attack my sister's body. From that day forward, God equipped Lissy with knowledge of the Bible and a gift of faith she exercises when she prays for others who are oppressed by Satan. In times of crisis, she still mobilizes our family to pray and leads us in victory over spiritual darkness. God is powerfully using her in North India as the wife of a faithful national leader, Pastor P. D. Joseph. Through

Immediately, the rain stopped where we were conducting the meeting. We continued worshipping. Many people received Christ that evening.

her ministries of hospitality, prayer, caring, and giving God uses her to restore and deliver needy families.

Up to—and especially during the year 1983—when my siblings and I lived together and attended church in Thiruvananthapuram, God revealed the truth of His Word to each of them. One by one, they obeyed Christ, accepted Him as Lord and Savior, and followed Him in baptism. Consequently, we longed for others to know about Jesus. Whenever we could, we traveled to other villages to share the Gospel of Christ.

One evening we held an open air meeting in front of the house of a family closely related to my father. Many village people came to hear the message and to watch us from the street. While we were worshipping, it started to rain. Undaunted, we continued the service. In faith and simple prayer, we asked God to show His power by stopping the rain so unbelievers would see His power and believe. Immediately, the rain stopped where we were conducting the meeting. We continued worshipping. Many people received Christ that evening. Through that experience, my faith in God increased and the villagers not only respected the God I worshipped, but grew to trust me as a spiritual leader.

As the years passed, my father began to soften a little in his dealings with me, even allowing me to visit home. During that time, my mother gave her life to Christ. Not long after she accepted Christ, she and I visited her birthplace together. We learned that an evangelist was preaching and a baptism was scheduled for the next day. I urged my mother to obey Christ by being baptized. When she was baptized, she removed all of her ornaments—a practice common for new believers in our area as a testimony to their new Christian faith.

When we arrived home the next day, my father immediately noticed that my mother had removed all of her ornaments—including her *tali,* a marriage necklace with a fine gold chain and thin cross pendant. He was furious! To him, this was an overt act of rejecting him and their marriage covenant. He beat my mother until she writhed in pain on the floor. The brutal anger he unleashed on her was unbearable to watch. She silently accepted this suffering for Christ and, to this day, God has honored her sacrifice and unwavering faith. Out of these life experiences have grown gifts of understanding, compassion, love, care, and hospitality. These gifts draw many village women to our family home. God uses my mother to touch these hurting people and, with the passing of years, impact the world for Christ.

> **Suffering produces character, strengthens faith, and glorifies Christ.**

The collective experiences of my family and my life have taught me not to be afraid of suffering for Christ. If we are living out our calling in Christ, we will suffer. Jesus Himself said, *"I have told you these things, so that in me you may have peace. In this world you will have trouble. But take heart! I have overcome the world"* (John 16:33). Suffering produces character, strengthens faith, and glorifies Christ. Suffering for His sake does not snuff out His light, but causes it to burn brighter. When we suffer, we identify with the Lord in His suffering. I have learned the truth of Philippians 1:29, *"For to you it has been granted on behalf of Christ, not only to believe in him, but also to suffer for his sake."* We are blessed when we are persecuted for His name. In the Beatitudes, Christ teaches us the principle, *"Blessed are you when they revile and persecute you, and say all kinds of evil against you falsely for my sake. Rejoice and be exceedingly glad, for great is your reward in heaven, for so they persecuted the prophets who were before you"* (Matthew 5: 11-12).

During my years in the city, I matured in my role as the spiritual head of my family. I saw firsthand that Christ's power is sufficient to overthrow every stronghold of Satan. He delivered my family from darkness. This same power is for all people who believe in Him and call upon His name. Satan's grip on South Asia is prevalent and palpable. His work is less conspicuous and more subtle in the West. In both regions His goal is the same—to destroy homes, churches, and nations. Christ is the only answer. Jesus is calling out and building up an obedient people for Himself—a people who know Him and are willing to suffer for Him. It is a joy to reflect on how He has worked out His purpose in my life, the life of my family, and the lives of those around us. Looking back, I see how He was building and defining my place among His people—to be a servant-leader willing to suffer for His Gospel and battle against the schemes of Satan. Of course, I didn't realize it at the time, but God was planting that same vision in the heart of my future wife. He was preparing our hearts to receive one another, to work alongside each other in ministry, and to be willing to suffer in our pursuit of His purpose for our lives.

6

SHE IS GOOD FOR YOU

"By all means marry; if you get a good wife, you'll be happy. If you get a bad one, you'll become a philosopher."

~ Socrates

"*She is good for you*," was the statement uttered by my grandfather in the summer of 1986 after meeting my wife, Moni, for the first time. I wholeheartedly agreed. Moni grew up in Queens, New York with her two brothers and two sisters. Her father is a good man and worked many years with the Kerala State Agricultural Department while her mother managed the home.

Moni, already established in the Christian faith, was praying for a God-fearing, tall, handsome, young man who was full of energy and ambition.

Moni's maternal uncles moved to the States many years before. This led Moni's family to immigrate to the U.S. in 1979. Moni was fourteen years old when she arrived in New York.

In 1986, when she was twenty-one, Moni and her family came back to India for the marriages of her two brothers—and possibly her own. Moni's family received many marriage recommendations for her through various pastors who knew the family well. Moni, already established in the Christian faith, was praying for a God-fearing, tall, handsome young man who was full of energy and ambition. I was praying for a godly woman who would become a suitable partner in ministry with me. I was twenty-six, ready to marry, and prayed eagerly.

On a Tuesday morning in early August 1986, I got up early to bathe and shave. I felt something special was about to take place, but I wasn't exactly sure what. At about ten o'clock, three men came to the door, including Moni's brother Benjamin, to invite me to their church and following the worship service, their home to meet Moni.

I was thrilled, yet my main goal was to catch a glimpse of this woman, Moni.

The next Sunday, my friend Jayadevan and I took a bus to Pathanapuram. We were late and headed straight to the church. By the time we arrived, the worship service had already started. I had met the pastor, Alexander, at other meetings. He greeted me and asked me to share my testimony to exhort the people. I was thrilled, yet my main goal was to catch a glimpse of this woman, Moni. I passionately shared my story with the believers and read my favorite Scripture passage, Psalm 4:7-8. There were many beautiful women in the room and I scanned the crowd wondering which one was Moni.

After the church service, Moni's family invited us to their home for lunch. Moni served us lemonade. It was a good time but crowded and busy. Many family members and friends had come to meet me. Finally, I freed myself from the commotion and took Moni's uncle aside. I asked him to give me half-an-hour to talk with Moni privately. He was gracious and kind to grant my request.

Taking Moni aside into a small room, I sat down with her and shared my heart. I listened carefully as she shared her heart for ministry. I shared my testimony and told her of my family responsibilities. She shared about her life in New York, her university studies, and her involvement in her local church. She was born in Pathanapuram, about twenty-five miles from my village and came from a strong Christian family background. She related that, years ago, her grandfather accepted Jesus and became a street preacher. He was a highly respected man of God. During her childhood years in India, Moni accepted Christ through Vacation Bible School at her local church. She told me of her family's immigration to America in 1979 when she was fourteen and described their first home in Queens, New York.

I was impressed and immediately liked her. I believe I was drawn to her because of the Holy Spirit. He knew we were right for each other. From somewhere deep inside, words began to form in my heart. Before I knew it, they made their way past my vocal chords. I told her, "I love you." In our culture, one does not say, "I love you," unless it is genuine. I was courageous and claimed her by faith for my life. I hardly knew anything about her family, but had instantly liked her parents. In a short time, we heard a knock on the door and one of Moni's relatives entered, motioning to us that our time was up. I had only spoken with Moni for thirty minutes but knew she was God's gift chosen for me!

After meeting Moni that Sunday, I went to my parents' home and described her to them. Even though I loved Moni, my parents' permission and blessings were vital. In response to my request for their blessing, my immediate family members, including my grandfather and my father's uncle, went to see Moni and interviewed her. Afterwards, the family consensus was that they liked her too. They commented that she was gentle, innocent, and beautiful. My grandpa told me after meeting Moni, "Saji, I am eighty years old. I want to tell you that she is good for you." Because he was the most respected person in our family, Grandpa's approval and blessing was the sign of confirmation for further action towards engagement.

In our culture, marriage is not just between two individuals. It is a relationship between two families. The next week, Moni's family came to our home. After meeting together, there was general approval on both sides. The engagement function was at Moni's home on August 19, 1986. About three-hundred people attended. Because of the many relatives we needed to greet, Moni and I had almost no opportunity to talk. We were both disappointed.

On August 26, 1986, the marriage ceremony was held in a rented auditorium in my hometown of Ayur. Adorned in her wedding dress, Moni traveled four tedious hours to get there. The wedding service lasted another two hours and included preaching—from both sides of the family—as well as the marriage ceremony itself. Immediately following the service we, according to cultural norms, visited Moni's home for a few days. We also visited family and traveled to a few cities in South India with Moni's newly married brother, William. After a short month, Moni had to leave for New York to continue her job and her studies. The separation was hard but we endured.

> **Because he was the most respected person in our family, Grandpa's approval and blessing was the sign of confirmation for further action towards engagement.**

During the ensuing months, I continued to cry out to God for the salvation of my father. Even though he was ignorant of biblical truths, he had always shown compassion towards the poor and weak. He often brought people from the streets into our home and asked my mother to feed them. I learned the value of compassion from him. Even though he brutally persecuted me, my father is the man I respect most in my life—my hero. He gave me life, provided for my growth, and opened the doors of education to me in spite of his lack of resources.

Although my father did not support my new found faith, he appreciated the godly changes in all his children. He often shared with his extended family and friends the changes he witnessed. His heart slowly moved towards God. Whenever my siblings and I traveled to my parents' village to conduct evangelistic meetings, my father, who was curious, came and listened to the speakers. God used the messages he heard to soften his heart and move him towards a commitment to Christ.

People of all faiths attended our evangelistic meetings. The whole Gospel was boldly preached and God's faithfulness protected everyone from demonic influence. Many of my city friends traveled with me to my home village and shared how Jesus had transformed their lives. I watched a genuine change take place among members of my extended family and my neighbors. They listened intently during Bible studies. Their interest in prayer deepened. Village children and youth attended our Sunday School classes and were thrilled to hear Bible stories. In those days spiritual famine and hunger for God's Word were pervasive. People readily received the Truth because it so powerfully addressed their personal longings as well as prevalent social evils such as alcoholism, corruption, and family dysfunction.

One of our main motives for holding regular meetings was for my father to hear the Truth. Consequently, when I preached in different locations, I asked my brothers and sisters in Christ to join me in praying for his salvation. Our immediate family fasted and prayed for him to make a genuine commitment to Christ. Every time I visited my father, I told him, "Daddy, I will be restless until you follow Christ." This statement touched his heart. Even so, his family background, traditions, and fear of his elders and priests made him unwilling to leave his traditions. He did not yet realize that church traditions would not save him. Only faith in Jesus alone can do that. Like many in the world today, he did not grasp God's Truth. Unless we boldly follow Christ, our testimony will not be strong. Christ's call is a radical call! Jesus demands complete loyalty to Him alone. The Bible says, *"If anyone comes to me and does not hate his father and mother, wife and children, brothers and sisters, yes, and his own life also, he cannot be my disciple"* (Luke 14:26).

As I continued evangelizing and teaching in Thiruvanthapuram, Moni and I communicated by letter, and often, a weekly phone call she made from New York. Because I didn't have a phone, she called my neighbor's house. I ran there excited to just hear her voice.

Every time I visited my father, I told him, "Daddy, I will be restless until you follow Christ."

The six months passed by slowly for us. Finally, she returned to India for a month-long visit. It was during that whirlwind month that I really got to know her. We traveled together and had a wonderful time visiting friends and various places.

One of our visits was to the hospital to see my grandpa who had, prior to Moni's visit, suffered a brain injury in a motorbike accident. It was a very sad time. Moni and I had hoped he would live until we could both visit him together. When we arrived, my grandpa was unconscious. The doctors said there was no hope for recovery. Even so, when Moni spoke to him and offered him water to drink, he regained consciousness, drank the water, and gripped her hand tightly. That was the last time he responded to anyone. He died within a few days. Two years prior to his death, Grandpa trusted Christ while visiting me in the city. He obeyed Jesus in baptism and became a living testimony to the people in his community of the life-changing power of Christ. Many family members thought Grandpa would never come to the Lord. But God is faithful. Grandpa was completely transformed. He regularly walked many miles to attend a local church and often shared the hope he'd found in Christ with members of his extended family. We know he is enjoying eternity with the Lord.

After grandpa's funeral, Moni returned to the United States. Once again, it was hard for me. I went with her to the airport and wept as she walked towards the plane. Eight months later, in April 1988, I received my visa permitting me to travel to America and reunite with Moni. As I was preparing to leave India, the Holy Spirit prompted me to go to my parents' home and spend quality time with my father. I sensed God urging me to confront him again with Biblical Truth and the good news about Jesus. Expectantly, I looked forward to a good weekend.

During this time with my parents, I reminded my father of God's faithfulness. He had blessed our lives by delivering our family from sickness, Satan, and demonic oppression. Christ's peace and joy overcame the darkness that once pervaded our home. These miracles could only come from God! I asked my father to consider the lives of those extended family members who had given their lives to Christ. I challenged him to compare the devastation of their previous existence with the transformed lives they were now living. Jesus had undeniably blessed and delivered them! I knew my father if he weighed this evidence, he would surely not deny these truths.

Until just a few months prior, my father argued that, by becoming a born again Christian, I had brought shame to the family and hindered Lissy's chances of finding a suitable husband. In our culture, if the eldest brother has a sister at home ready for marriage, he must first honor her by finding her a suitable life partner before he marries. However, I married first—promising Lissy I would not leave for the United States until I found a godly man for her. It wasn't long before God answered my prayer and honored my promise to Lissy. He brought Pastor P. D. Joseph into our lives—a man totally sold out for the Lord. Furthermore, God miraculously provided all the money needed for her wedding. On January 9, 1988— just three months before my departure—Lissy and Pastor P. D. Joseph were married. As I reminded my father of these powerful works of God in our family, I saw his heart changing.

> **"Daddy, I will be leaving soon for New York, and I do not know when we will see each other again."**

I finally confronted him saying, "Daddy, I will be leaving soon for New York, and I do not know when we will see each other again." I told him I had asked believers everywhere to pray for him. I asked, "Daddy, why are you not surrendering your life to Christ? Wherever I go I want to tell *everyone* that my *whole family* follows Christ, but I can't." This was his appointed moment. He broke down in tears, hugged me, and accepted Christ by praying the sinner's prayer. Hallelujah! Praise Jesus! We rejoiced, while heaven rejoiced with us!

The same weekend my father was converted, we arranged for his baptism in an uncle's family pool. We invited many to come and celebrate with us. I remember singing songs of praise as we walked the half mile from our house to the pool. Afterwards, the entire half mile back home, we sang songs and praised God for His goodness to us.

Many members of my father's extended family were not happy with his decision. They felt betrayed by him. The church priests removed our names from their register and asked us not to enter the church again. Even so, the Lord honored my dad before the people of his village by forever changing his life. Christ says in Matthew 10:32-33, *"Therefore whoever confesses me before men, him I will also confess before my Father who is in heaven. But whoever denies me before men, him I will also deny before my Father who is in heaven."* I am grateful that my father gave his life to Jesus and, to this day, confesses Christ before men as his Savior and Lord.

My father was the last member of my immediate family to give his life to Christ. My family became whole—each one a member of the family of God. As I prepared to leave India, I rejoiced that God had answered our prayers and honored our witness by paving the way for every member of my family to find new life in Jesus. Knowing that all was well with my family in India, I eagerly faced the future and my new life in America with confidence.

To this day, I often look in amazement at how God has blessed my life. He saved my family and gave me the gift of Moni. She has brought so much joy to me and my family. She is my parents' first daughter-in-law and is well-loved. She gained their love and respect by her godliness, love, and the care she shows to everyone in the family. She has a great sense of humor and is fun-loving. Whenever we gather together, it's not long before everyone is laughing. Her primary gift is hospitality and she excels in it. She possesses all the characteristics of the noble woman of Proverbs 31. She fears the Lord, works hard, and suffers with me in the ministry of the Gospel. We are single-minded in our purpose—to honor God. God has given me a true soul-mate in

Moni. She is His very special gift to me and to the ministry of RIMI!

PART II

MOVING TO THE LAND OF OPPORTUNITY

God is pursuing with omnipotent passion a worldwide purpose of gathering joyful worshippers for himself from every tribe and tongue and people and nation. He has an inexhaustible enthusiasm for the supremacy of his name among the nations. Therefore, let us bring our affections into line with his, and, for the sake of his name, let us renounce the quest for worldly comforts and join his global purpose.

~ John Piper

7

PURSUING GOD'S CALL

The Christian cannot be satisfied as long as any human activity
is either opposed to Christianity or out of connection with
Christianity. Christianity must pervade not merely all nations
but also all of human thought.

~ J. Gresham Machen

Two years after we were married, I was excited to, finally, join Moni in Queens, New York. I moved in with Moni and her family and began working with a title research company, but I could not get India's spiritual need out of my mind. Time and time again the Lord reminded me of the moment in India when I surrendered my life to serve Him wholeheartedly. With every passing day in Queens, my passion to minister in my homeland grew. God worked in my heart, preparing me to do His will. I began to get involved in South Asian churches around the city. I was determined to remind my countrymen of the spiritual need that remained in our native land.

I also struggled greatly as I contemplated what God's will was for my life. In Asia, the cultural norm is for the oldest son to take care of his parents and younger siblings. For this reason, I was grateful to be able to work and send money back to India. Still, the work was not fulfilling. If I obeyed God's call, I would have to give up my financial security—most likely jeopardizing my extended family's welfare—and give up my American Dream. I had to decide between materialism or following God's call.

During this time of struggle, God's Word gripped my heart. I sensed Him calling me into missions as I read and contemplated I John 2:15-17, *"Do not love the world or the things in the world. If anyone loves the world, the love of the Father is not in him. For all that is in the world – the lust of the flesh, the lust of the eyes, and the pride of life – it is not of the Father but is of the world. And the world is passing away and the lust of it; but he who does the will of God abides forever."* These words resounded in my mind and heart for six months. Finally, I knew what I had to do. Deep down, I knew God's purpose for my life involved more than accumulating material things. I recalled how happy and fulfilled I had been in India when I was sharing my testimony with unbelievers. I soon realized

> **Once I grasped the promise that God would take full responsibility for my family, I made plans and prepared to obey His calling.**

where God wanted me. Despite this understanding, however, my burden for my family weighed on me. I cried out to God, "Who will take care of my family if I go?" In a clear, distinct voice, He replied, *"I will."* God reminded me that He is sovereign and that my family were His children too. He would take care of them.

Since those defining moments, I have embraced the truth of Matthew 6:31, *"Therefore, do not worry, saying, 'What shall we eat?' or 'What shall we drink?' or 'What shall we wear?'... For your Heavenly Father knows that you need all these things. But seek first the kingdom of God and His righteousness, and, all these things shall be added to you. Therefore, do not worry about tomorrow..."*

Once I grasped the promise that God would take full responsibility for my family, I made plans and prepared to obey His calling. I decided to attend seminary so I could deepen my faith, increase my knowledge of God's Word, and later, impart what I learned to my fellow South Asians.

Wondering which seminary I should attend, I wrote Ravi Zacharias, a prominent apologist from India based in Atlanta, and asked his advice. He suggested I attend Trinity Evangelical Divinity School (TEDS) in Deerfield, Illinois, located about an hour north of Chicago. Established in 1897 and affiliated with the Evangelical Free Church of America, I found Trinity's mission statement—*to raise up leaders... to provide theological leadership for the global church of Jesus Christ*—fit my calling. I didn't know anyone in Chicago and had never been there before. But I trusted God's promises and stepped out in faith believing Hebrews 13:5, *"Keep your lives free from the love of money and be content with what you have, because God has said, 'Never will I leave you; never will I forsake you.'"*

Moni fully supported my decision in spite of the drastic changes it required—including a move from Queens, New York to Deerfield, Illinois. Initially, her family was reluctant to support our decision. They were concerned because of my family responsibilities in India. After a time, however, they understood my resolve and blessed us in our pursuit of God's calling on our lives.

By then I had saved 3,000 dollars. Moni and I flew to Chicago and I enrolled at TEDS. We bought our first car, a used Oldsmobile Cutlass, for $2,700 and I prepared to start my studies in the fall of 1988.

8

LIFE IN THE WINDY CITY

"Whenever you are asked if you can do a job, tell 'em,
'Certainly I can!' Then get busy and find out how to do it."

~ *Theodore Roosevelt*

God is faithful when we follow His will for our lives. I knew no one when we moved to Chicago, but God was preparing a place for Moni and me to live. Before we arrived, I was given the phone number of a person living in Waukegan. Kurien turned out to be one of my former business students from India. When I called, he immediately recognized my voice. For two weeks, Kurien and his wife graciously opened up their small apartment to Moni and me until we found an apartment of our own. By arranging this contact with one of my former business students, God confirmed to me that we were walking in His will. We will always be grateful to Kurien and his wife for their hospitality. To this day, they remain faithful supporters of RIMI.

In the weeks that followed, I worked hard—taking on several part-time jobs. Moni also worked to help support us. There were times when we were financially short but, in the end, God always provided for our needs. One semester I could not register for classes because

I had no money for tuition. At the same time, I spent a week in the hospital because of high blood pressure. Moni recalls that I cried like a baby, "Moni, my head hurts!" News of my hospitalization traveled around Trinity's campus and the seminary family began to pray for me. God answered by restoring my health and meeting our financial needs. Following my hospitalization, Trinity offered me a partial scholarship.

During my four years at Trinity, God continued to press the spiritual needs of Indian people upon my heart. He continued to both intensify and clarify His calling on my life. I knew God was calling me to missions almost from the moment of my conversion. But now at seminary—as I learned and understood more of His Word—He was progressively revealing the details of His plans for my life. God assured me, as He assures every believer that *"We are his workmanship, created in Christ Jesus for good works, which God prepared beforehand that we should walk in them"* (Ephesians 2:10).

The continuous study of God's Word showed me a systematic, panoramic view of Biblical history and how God includes us in His eternal purposes. My classes, the chapel services I attended, and my personal devotions brought me to a clearer understanding of God's Word and deepened my desire to see all people come to a saving knowledge of His grace. The Prophet Isaiah articulated what I was discovering about God's purpose in the proclamation of His Word, *"So shall my word be that goes forth from my mouth; It shall not return to me void, But it shall accomplish what I please, and it shall prosper in the thing for which I sent it"* (Isaiah 55:11).

> **"We are his workmanship, created in Christ Jesus for good works, which God prepared beforehand that we should walk in them" (Ephesians 2:10).**

Becoming acquainted with members of Trinity's faculty—and hearing their life stories—enriched my vision. They were, and are, godly people whose lives testify of God's goodness and grace. Under their tutorage my faith grew and the philosophy of missions that gave birth to RIMI evolved. I fondly remember Dr. Robert Coleman, who gathered a few students in his office at 5:30 a.m. each week. Together we studied the book of Revelation. On our knees we passionately read Scripture, listened, and prayed. Dr. Coleman enabled us to catch a glimpse of heaven. More than that, he created within us a longing for the lost to enter into God's and heaven's glories.

God used the self-sacrificing lives of such faithful mentors to change our lives. They were, and remain, God's agents of transformation. They are a part of that great cloud of witnesses mentioned in Hebrews 12:1, *"Therefore, since we are surrounded by such a great cloud of witnesses, let us throw off everything that hinders and the sin that so easily entangles, and let us run with perseverance the race marked out for us."*

But faculty members were not the only mentors I had at Trinity. My seminary training included time in campus libraries where I was introduced to many faithful men and women of the past. Hearing and reading the stories of these great missionaries gave me a sense of my place in God's global cause. The paths these saints traveled inspired me to faithfully run the race marked out for me (Hebrews 12:1). As I read, I soaked up the vision God gave each of them. Their lives encouraged me as God continued to confront me with what He wanted me to do in South Asia and beyond. As I lived, worked, and studied, their words accompanied me:

"Nothing so clears the vision and lifts up the life, as a decision to move forward in what you know to be entirely the will of the Lord" (John Paton, missionary to the New Hebrides).

"Oh, that I had a thousand lives and a thousand bodies! All of them should be devoted to no other employment but to preach Christ" (Robert Moffat, missionary to Africa).

"You sons of England, here is a field for your energies. Bring with you your highest education and greatest talents; you will find scope for the exercise of them all. You men of God, who have resolved to devote your lives to the cure of the souls of men, here is the proper field for you. It is not to win numbers to a Church, but to win men to the Saviour, and who otherwise will be lost, that I entreat you to leave your work at home to the many who are ready to undertake it, and to come forth yourselves to reap this field now white to the harvest" (Alexander Mackay, missionary to Uganda, Africa).

"We must be global Christians with a global vision because our God is a global God" (John Stott).

"It is my desire to show my attachment to the cause of Him who died for me by devoting my life to His service" (David Livingston, missionary to Africa).

"You have been saying much about Dr. Carey and his work. When I am gone, say nothing about Dr. Carey; speak about Dr. Carey's Saviour" (William Carey, missionary to India).

Befriending fellow students from around the world confirmed my call by connecting me to an exciting network of global thinkers and visionaries—each pursuing God's missionary purpose for their lives. While at TEDS I became the president of the International Student Fellowship. While serving in this position I was able to see God's Global Church up close. Students came to Trinity from all over the world and from all walks of life for one reason—to deepen their knowledge and relationship with God so they could better share the Good News with the lost. The following words express it well:

"We must be global Christians with a global vision because our God is a global God" (John Stott).

"World missions was on God's mind from the beginning" (Dave Davidson).

"But you, dear friends, build yourselves up in your most holy faith and pray in the Holy Spirit" (Jude 1:20).

Relating to Indians in Chicago kept God's vision for South Asia in the forefront of my mind. I worked to mobilize South Asians, especially Indians, living in the Chicago area. I organized annual meetings and fellowships to raise awareness of the spiritual needs of India. I also raised money to help meet the financial needs of indigenous missionaries serving there. As I worked in Chicago to mobilize other Indian believers, I sought to live out the words of Ephesians 6:18, *"And pray in the Spirit on all occasions with all kinds of prayers and requests. With this in mind, be alert and always keep on praying for all the saints."*

During my four years of study at Trinity, God prepared me for the work I would be doing with RIMI. Looking back, I clearly see how His hand provided for and guided Moni and I. It is wonderful to remember how faithful our God is to His children.

9

GIVE ME INDIA OR LET ME DIE

I have great sorrow and unceasing anguish in my heart. For I could wish that I myself were cursed and cut off from Christ for the sake of my brothers, those of my own race.

~ Romans 9:2-3

Although I was able to make a difference during my time at Trinity, my heart and mind were focused on the bigger picture. I literally kept the vision God gave me before my eyes by mounting a large map of India on my bedroom wall. Above it, I posted my personal version of John Knox's prayer. The great Scottish preacher cried out to God, *"Give me, O Lord, Scotland, or I die!"* Above my map of India I wrote, *"Give me India, or let me die!"* This was and is how intense my prayer for India was and continues to be. Each day I laid my hand on every Indian state and prayed, "God send me to all these places." It is worth noting that God has sent me to 26 of 28 Indian states so far. God is moving towards fully answering my prayer.

I believe God powerfully responds to prayer. The Bible demonstrates this from beginning to end. In the Old and New Testaments, prayer's potency is central to all God does in and through believers. James exhorts us, *"Therefore confess your sins to each other and pray for each other so that you may be healed. The prayer of a righteous man is powerful and effective"*

(James 5:16). John promises, *"...we can be confident that he will listen to us whenever we ask him for anything in line with his will"* (I John 5:14).

Consider how the power of faith and prayer is demonstrated in Paul's life. Acts 28:7-9 says, *"There was an estate nearby that belonged to Publius, the chief official of the island. He welcomed us to his home and for three days entertained us hospitably. His father was sick in bed, suffering from fever and dysentery. Paul went in to see him and, after prayer, placed his hands on him and healed him. When this had happened, the rest of the sick on the island came and were cured"* (Acts 28:7-9).

> **Above my map of India I wrote, "Give me India, or let me die!"**

With this same faith and intensity, I passionately prayed for my native country. Out of a deep longing in my heart, I cried out—and still cry out—for the salvation of South Asia! Like Paul, I am resting on God's promise that if we ask anything according to His will in Christ's name, He will answer. S. D. Gordon put it this way, *"You can do more than pray after you have prayed, but you cannot do more than pray until you have prayed…. Prayer is striking the winning blow…service is gathering up the results."*

To prepare for my ministry in South Asia, not only did I specifically and intently pray—I also gathered information about each Indian state and collected it in a binder. The more I learned about India's needs the more passionate I became to see my fellow South Asians saved. The statistics I gathered about India broke my heart:

- 4,635 distinct people groups, spread over a geographic area one-third the size of the U.S.A.

- 6,400 castes, each functions as a separate group because of social barriers

- 1,652 languages, with 18 major languages

- 38% literacy, mostly women and children

- 80% Hindu; 12% Muslim; 2.4% Christians (but less than 1% in North India); 2% Sikh; 1% Buddhist

- 300 million middle class people; 600 million live in poverty; 300 million live below the bread-line

- 70% of the Indian population lives in 600,000 rural villages

I began to share this information with people in the United States. My goal was to make American believers aware of the spiritual and physical needs faced by our South Asian brothers and sisters. I entreated as many people as possible to join me in the vision God was laying on my heart. Then, when His time came, we would be ready to mobilize, return to South Asia, and establish the ministry God was calling us to—a ministry of meeting needs by shining God's light into the darkness.

10

AMERICA'S KINDESS AND GENEROSITY

*God has given us two hands, one to receive with
and the other to give with.*

~ *Billy Graham*

I am certain there are Christians and non-Christians who would disagree with me when I say that America is a kind and compassionate country—but I have witnessed it firsthand. I clearly saw the beauty of American believers when God used them to meet my needs. There were days when we did not know from where the next meal would come. But God was always faithful and provided for us through the giving of others. Some left baskets of food outside our door. Others stuffed large amounts of money in my seminary mailbox. Seldom did we know who gave these gifts to us. We were unable to say "thanks" to those God used to meet our needs. They gave secretly, and they gave in love. They gave because God had first given them the greatest gift of all—forgiveness and new life in Christ. The givers had no desire to be recognized. Still, we are truly grateful to God for the faithfulness and generosity of these servants of His.

When we reflect on our years at Trinity, we see how God in His love continually provided for our financial needs. Moni was hired to help manage the seminary cafeteria. Because of her employment, my tuition was discounted. She did not have to work Saturdays or Sundays, giving us the flexibility we needed to travel on weekends and share our vision. The partial scholarship from Trinity was both a blessing and a relief. At that time we were living primarily on Moni's income. Late at night, we both worked for a cleaning service. All these provisions enabled me to complete my seminary education, which provided me

> **From the beginning, I have asked the Global Church to "hold the ropes" for our ministry in South Asia. They have responded with compassion and joined us in the vision.**

with the skills I would later need to reach out to South Asians all over the world. By God's grace, I graduated debt-free. I am so grateful to Him!

The Bible commands us to love each other and reach out with generosity. In God's Word we see the church striving to live together in community—actively loving one another for God's glory. Acts 4:32-35 paints a picture of God's design for His Church, *"All the believers were one in heart and mind. No one claimed that any of his possessions was his own, but they shared everything they had. With great power the apostles continued to testify to the resurrection of the Lord Jesus, and much grace was with them all. There were no needy persons among them. For from time to time those who owned lands or houses sold them, brought the money from the sales and put it at the apostles' feet, and it was distributed to anyone as he had need."*

In my experience, I have found the lives of many American believers reflect this picture of Christian love and community. I am grateful for this dedication to serving God through kindness, generosity, and meeting the needs of the Body of Christ. I pray the American Church will continue to reflect the heart of Jesus in this way for years to come! As the ministry of RIMI has grown into what it is today, I have looked to the generosity of American believers and churches for support. I continue to look to that generosity today. William Carey once heard someone remark, "There is a gold mine in India, but it seems almost as deep as the center of the earth. Who will venture to explore it?" He answered, "I will venture to go down, but remember that you must hold the ropes." From the beginning, I have asked the Global Church to "hold the ropes" for our ministry in South Asia. They have responded with compassion and joined us in the vision.

It still amazes me when I see the partnership God has knit together between RIMI and the Western Church. It is through such partnerships that God promises to fulfill the Great Commission and glorify Himself in places like South Asia. In fact, it was the birth of this wholehearted partnership between RIMI and Western believers that enabled us to take another "leap of faith"—propelling us into the next stage of life and ministry God had called us to.

PART III

MOVING AHEAD WITH GOD'S VISION

Vision is the art of seeing things invisible.

~ Jonathan Swift

The Lukos Family - The entire Lukos family accepted Christ and served the Lord in different parts of India.

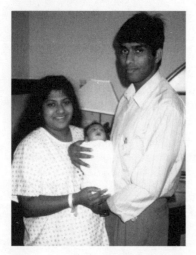

The Birth of daughter Maryann

Saji and Moni's marriage

Theological Seminary Campus in Nagpur, Central India

11

THE YEAR OF TWO BIRTHS

*"Faith never knows where it is being led, but it loves
and knows the One who is leading."*

~ *Oswald Chambers*

My first task in establishing the ministry was formulating a plan
for Moni and I to travel back to India to discover the specifics
of God's plan. We had an intense desire to reach out to our fellow
South Asians, but we had not yet discovered how to do it. Ironically,
in all my years growing up in India, I had never been outside of my
own state. Most of what I knew about India came by way of research,
reading, and meeting people. While that knowledge gave birth to my
vision, it was not enough to bring the vision to fruition. I needed to
travel extensively and encounter the whole of India and her people.
God impressed upon my heart that I must again walk the streets of my
homeland. On her soil, I must prayerfully commit all future action to
God and His glory!

Along with the excitement of planning and preparing to return to
India, Moni and I desired to start a family. Several years had now passed
since our wedding and God had not blessed us with a child. In South
Asia, the expectation is that couples should have a child by their second

year of marriage. While our parents were disappointed, the absence of a child was hardest on Moni. Blaming the wife for childlessness is understood to be wrong in South Asian Christian homes. However, the tendency to do so still lingers as a cultural mind-set.

We dealt with our disappointment in the same way we always deal with difficult situations—we prayed. Moni's parents, my parents, our extended family, our friends and our church family prayed too. Our circle of faith was large as we asked God to give us a child. Because God's response to our pleas is always in keeping with His good and perfect plans for us, we trusted in His wisdom as we prayed and waited for His answer.

Because God's response to our pleas is always in keeping with His good and perfect plans for us, we trusted in His wisdom as we prayed and waited for His answer.

In the meantime, Moni and I both held many part-time jobs—working hard to earn enough money to return to India. Every day during the previous four years I had placed my hand on that map of India and prayed for my country. The desire to return burned deep in my heart!

On Mother's Day in 1992, we attended a church service at Glenview Evangelical Free Church. The pastor preached from 1 Samuel, relating how Hannah had prayed earnestly for a child. At the end of the service he asked the mothers in the congregation to stand up and receive a flower. Then the pastor asked those who wished to be mothers to stand up, and in faith, also receive a flower. Moni stood up and prayed silently, "Lord, I want to be a mom this time next year."

Moni will relate the story of how God answered our prayers:

When I was in high school, a man named Pastor Thomas visited my uncle's church in New York. After meeting me, he said to me, 'As soon as you complete your twenty-first year, God will take you in a new direction, give you a great ministry, your family will be amazed, and your name will be known all over the world.'

The years passed and I forgot about what Pastor Thomas had said about my life. It all came back to me, however, when in 1992, Saji and I stopped at a friend's house for a prayer meeting. As I was coming down the stairs, I recognized Pastor Thomas sitting in a nearby chair. I had this fleeting thought, 'He is the pastor from that meeting back in high school!' As I sat down, I recalled his words about my future. Since his prophecy, I had married at the age of twenty-one. Now, Saji and I were preparing for ministry back in India. It was all happening just as he had prophesied. Could the Lord also have a child in mind for us? God knew my thoughts. The thought had barely entered my mind when Pastor Thomas got up from his chair. He came to where I sat—followed by his wife who had been sitting on the other side of the room. He placed his hand on my forehead. His wife placed hers on my stomach. They prayed for me and our future child, saying, 'We rebuke Satan's scheme of preventing a future generation!' That happened in early November. A few months later I became pregnant!

Soon, we had earned and saved enough money to take a trip back to India. Both Saji and I were excited to be heading back home. But on the way there I became very ill. When we arrived in India, I was hospitalized with a distended abdomen. I asked them to check to see if I was pregnant, but for some reason they kept dismissing that possibility. Eventually, however, they did a pregnancy test. As the doctor passed Saji in the hallway, he told him that he was going to be a father. Saji immediately called my mother in New York. She was overjoyed!

Later, my mother told me that they had been praying that God would give us a child. She also told me that God had confirmed to her just months before that Saji and I would be having a child.

We decided I should return to the States before I got too far along in the pregnancy so no harm would come to the baby during the flight. Before I left India, I had a dream everything back in Chicago had changed. I was still working as a supervisor in Trinity's cafeteria, but the people were different. Everything was different. I shared this dream with Saji and he suggested that perhaps I was just nervous about going back to Chicago alone. I accepted his reasoning.

On my way home, I stopped in New York to see my family. While there, I called my Chicago manager. When I asked her how things were going, I mentioned my dream to her. She responded, 'Moni, your dream has come true. I no longer work there. New management is in charge.' She reassured me that the new supervisor was a very nice man who would be willing to give me back my job. I found this to be true.

I knew that just as God had been faithful to them in their ministries, He would be faithful to us in ours.

At first, I stayed with a friend on campus. I was waiting to see if I could get some housing there. The college informed me that no housing was available. I would have to wait until April for something to open up. I wasn't sure what was going to happen. I didn't know where I was going to live. It was a hard time because Saji was still back in India and I was alone. But once again, God took care of us.

My cousin in Chicago, John Varghese and wife Amy, opened their home to me. I moved in with them. He would get up early, take me to work at Trinity, and then drive to his own job. Living with his family was a joy. Even though I missed Saji greatly, I was never really lonely."

Once Moni—pregnant with our first child—returned to the United States, I set out on my journey of discovery across India. I initially planned my itinerary based on contacts I had with friends from my home state. Mainly government employees and church planters, they lived in various places throughout India. While staying with them, they taught me about their geographical areas and introduced me to their friends and acquaintances. From each of them I gathered information about the spiritual needs in their areas. The network of relationships I established enabled me to visit almost every state in India.

As I ventured across South Asia, God reminded me again of the legacy built by faithful missionary workers who preceded me. As I met believers from various denominations—visiting clinics, hospitals, children's homes, and churches—I realized I was not the first missionary to my country, nor would I be the last. In the past, God has used many faithful men and women to share the Good News of Christ with the people of South Asia. I ravenously studied the lives of these early church planters and leaders! I was anxious to visit the areas where they lived and worked. I wanted to see if their legacy continued. I drew strength and encouragement from their stories. I knew just as God had been faithful to them in their ministries, He would be faithful to us in ours.

Described below are the stories of some of the faithful missionaries whose lives inspired me as I traveled and learned of their service and sacrifice for Christ.

Pandita Ramabai,

April 23, 1858 - April 5, 1922

Ramabai, a godly woman whose social reform has been recognized by both the English and Indian governments, was an Indian Christian who translated the Bible into her native tongue of Marathi. She also wrote works that championed the cause of emancipation for Indian women. She traveled widely visiting England in 1883 and the United States from 1886 through 1888.

She established Mukti Mission in 1889 to provide refuge for young widows being abused by their families. The word, "Mukti," means "freedom" in the Marathi language. The Pandita Ramabai Mukti Mission still exists today—providing housing, education, training, and medical services for widows, orphans, the blind, and others in need.

During my travels, I met church planting couples who had been physically and spiritually nurtured at the Mukti Mission. Pastors' wives have grown up in the shelter and ministry of these homes. Now, strong in Christ, they minister with their husbands in un-reached places.

Ramabai's compassion for the poor, especially women, challenged me to take the bold step of nurturing women to become leaders in ministry. After learning how the servants at Mukti Mission care for the daily needs of hurting people, I resolved that RIMI would minister both to people's physical and spiritual needs.

Ida Scudder

December 9, 1870 – May 24, 1960

Ida Scudder was a medical missionary to India and the founder of the Christian Medical College in Vellore, near Chennai. Ida was born to Dr. John Scudder II and Mrs. Sophia Weld Scudder in 1870. She was one in a long line of medical missionaries. Initially, she did not want to become a medical missionary. She left India but, when her mother fell ill, returned to help her father.

In 1890, when Ida was twenty, she had an extraordinary experience that convinced her God wanted her to become a doctor and minister to the women of India. One evening, three men approached her as she studied at home. They asked her to come and help their young wives who were having difficulty giving birth. She offered to send her father since he was doctor. The husbands, however, refused to allow a man to see their wives. Ida was young, had no medical training, and was afraid to get involved. She did not go to help. The next morning she learned that all three women died during childbirth. Devastated, she resolved to become a doctor and minister in India. She declined

The next morning she learned that all three women died during childbirth. Devastated, she resolved to become a doctor and minister in India.

to be married to an American millionaire and instead attended Cornell Medical College in New York City. Her class (1899) was the first to graduate female medical students. Because of her academic achievement, Ida received a $10,000 grant. In 1900, she used the money to open a medical dispensary in Vellore. Two years later, she opened the Mary Taber Schell Hospital.

In July 1918, Ida opened a medical school for women in Vellore. In 1945, the college was opened to men as well as women. In 2003, Vellore Christian Medical Center ranked as one of the largest Christian hospitals in the world. This medical school is one of the premier medical colleges in India.

Two doctors in my own family studied at Ida Scudder's hospital. One is now a medical missionary. The other is a doctor in a Christian hospital. As I saw the impact good medical care has on people's lives, I came to share Ida Scudder's vision of demonstrating God's love by ministering to people's medical needs. Ida also modeled the importance of empowering people through vocational training. I decided that offering people opportunities to learn and pass on vocational skills would become a part of RIMI's ministry.

Sadhu Sundar Singh

September 1889 – 1929

Sundar Singh is one of the most prominent figures in the history of missions in India. Singh was born in Rampur, northern India, in September 1889. He was raised in the Sikh faith by his very religious mother. By the age of 16, Singh had mastered *Veda*, the sacred books of Hinduism. He also received training from some Sadhus. Sadhus were men who forsook all worldly pleasures for the sake of Hinduism. In spite of his devotion to Hindu principles, Sundar also studied at a school run by British missionaries. Here he was introduced to the Bible.

When Sundar was 14 years old his mother died. His life changed dramatically! He tore his Bible apart and burned it. He threw stones at preachers and encouraged others to do the same. At the same time, however, he found no peace in his own religion. He began to consider suicide. Three days after burning his Bible, he awoke at 3 a.m. and cried out, "Oh God, if you do exist, show me the right way or I will kill myself!" Just before 5 a.m. he repeated his prayer. Suddenly, he saw a brilliant light. In the midst of the radiance Sundar saw the figure of Jesus. A voice speaking Hindi asked, "How much longer are you going to search for me? I have come to save you. You prayed for the right path. Why have you not followed it?" Sundar realized Jesus was alive! He fell on his knees and felt a peace he had never felt before. The vision disappeared but the joy lingered on.

Singh was baptized in 1905, at the age of 16, and decided to become a Sadhu Christian. As a Sadhu, he wore a yellow robe, lived by the charity of others, and maintained celibacy. Ostracized by his family, he left home and set out to share his newfound faith. Sundar lived a nomadic life traveling from village to village. He shared the Gospel throughout India, Nepal, Tibet, and Ceylon. He also visited and preached in Malaysia, Japan, China, Western Europe, Australia, and Israel. In the summer of 1929 Sundar Singh entered Tibet. He was never seen again.

Sundar Singh chose a life of simplicity and sacrifice for the sake of Christ's cause—to seek and save the lost. His example reminded me that answering Christ's call requires whole-hearted commitment. Sundar Singh's example challenged me to live a simple, more focused life—and, through RIMI, to call others to do the same. Today, our indigenous workers live such lives. They trust God to meet their daily needs, knowing that *"no one can serve two masters…"* (Matthew 6:24). Many Western believers are also choosing to simplify their lifestyles so they can partner with RIMI workers in God's global cause.

Thomas Mathews

February 9, 1944 - November 24, 2005

Dr. Thomas Matthews was a man who became a movement for God. His journey to faith began in southern India. He was a university student working on his Bachelor's of Science degree in Kerala. During his years at the university, Thomas drifted further and further from God. In spite of this, his mother continued to pray for him to come to faith in Christ. While at youth camp he accidentally fell into a dangerous whirlpool of a deep river. Struggling to survive in the swirling waters,

Thomas replied, "God who sent me here for His work has sent it." The landlord left bewildered and never came to ask for rent money again.

he cried out to his mother's God. He promised to serve Him if He would only spare his life. Suddenly, a man Thomas did not know rushed to his aid and rescued him. Immediately, Thomas left his university studies and committed his life to evangelistic work in North India. After receiving four months of Bible training, however, Thomas could find no mission agency willing to support him. Despite this lack of financial backing—and warnings that the state of Rajasthan was a hard and hostile mission field—he collected his personal belongings and made the journey to Rajasthan, 2000 miles north of his home. He was 19 years old!

In Rajasthan, Thomas was subjected to starvation and constant beatings. This, however, did not deter him from his mission. He was reluctant to write or share about his personal needs. He supported himself day to day by selling Hindi language Gospels in the streets and villages. The monthly rent for his room was fifteen rupees, about fifty cents, but for the first three months, he could not pay it. One night his landlord threatened to throw him out if his rent wasn't paid by morning. He spent the entire night praying. The next morning, before the landlord came to collect the money, the postman knocked at the door. He handed Thomas a money order for fifty rupees. It was a wonderful gift from the Lord! The landlord was surprised when Thomas handed him forty-five rupees for three months rent. He asked how he could get so much money overnight. Thomas replied, "God, who sent me here for His work, has sent it." The landlord left bewildered and never came to ask for rent money again.

Countless stories demonstrate God's faithfulness in the life of Thomas Mathews. However, he also suffered and prayed constantly for God to meet his daily needs. During long winter nights, Thomas' only protection from the cold was a kerosene stove. He kept a low flame burning throughout the night. Having no cot or mattress, he slept on the floor with only a bed sheet. These challenges pushed Thomas forward from village to village. For six months—until God provided a bicycle—he traveled on foot. God often provided for his needs through the generosity of others.

On one occasion, Thomas prayed for a deathly sick man and God instantly healed him. The man convinced Thomas to pursue his studies—and then paid his school expenses for a year. While continuing to travel and evangelize, Thomas was able to complete his bachelor's degree with distinction and was awarded the University Merit Scholarship. This enabled him to complete his master's degree and achieve the University Gold Medal.

When Thomas was awarded the University Grants Commission's Fellowship, he pursued and completed his Ph.D. in 1979. During the time of his educational pursuits, Thomas continued to devote himself to full-time Gospel work. When he completed his Ph.D., he was offered a teaching position at the university, but refused it to continue his pastoral work. His academic achievements did, however, open doors to a number of ministry opportunities in Rajasthan. During this time, Thomas married Mary, a woman from Kerala who shared his passion and vision for northern India.

In the midst of continued hardship and hunger, Mary's gift of leadership inspired Thomas in their ministry. They initially confined their work to the state of Rajasthan. Then, in December, 1980, Dr. Donald McGavran invited Thomas to a pastor's conference in Bharuch, Gujarat. McGavran challenged him to "launch out into the deep." During that small conference the Lord reminded Thomas of His promise to the New Testament church at Philadelphia, *"Behold, I have set before thee an open door, and no man can shut it"* (Revelation 3:8). Dr. McGavran's encouragement led Thomas to found the Native Missionary Movement. Today, it remains a vibrant missionary movement, having established more than 1000 churches and a Bible college. Thomas and Mary's children continue to multiply their legacy by mentoring new pastors.

During my 1993 journey of discovery, I was honored to visit Thomas. His dedication, faith, and sacrifice for the sake of the Gospel truly inspired me. His life and character personified Jesus and challenged me to sharpen my own life. Before his death in 2005, Thomas and Mary visited our home in Chicago, and Moni and I were privileged to wash the feet of these saints! They blessed us abundantly with their humility and wisdom.

As I continued my travels through India, I encountered other men and women who were fervent about reaching the lost for Christ. Totally surrendered to Christ, they lived in difficult circumstances and were often killed by enemies of the Gospel. It encouraged me to fellowship with believers whose faith journeys were similar to mine. I rejoiced in hearing how God had upheld and cared for each of them, even as He had cared for me. These men and women—and their testimonies—still encourage me today.

Exploring was seeing. As I traveled from one part of the country to the other, God opened my eyes and caused me to see India with His eyes. I experienced a vast array of languages, cultures, and subcultures. The sheer number of languages and subcultures that make up Indian society was daunting to me. But God granted me courage, a pioneer spirit, and a willingness to trust in His provision. He caused me to dream big, to ask big things of Him, and to know He answers prayer.

Not all my time was spent exploring the land. I also studied God's Word. Consequently, I grew in my relationship with Him. I came to further understand His plan for my life and ministry. For a couple of months I also taught at New India Bible College, founded by Fuller Graduate, Dr. Abraham Phillip. Dr. Phillip and I lived in the same city and became friends during the time I ran my business school. I remember the words he spoke to me after my wedding, "Son, don't be deceived by America. Come back to India." Later, from his death bed, he wrote me again and made the same plea, "Come back to India." It was an honor to spend time with Dr. Phillip during my brief time at New India Bible College. I still cherish the memory of my ordination to the ministry while I was there.

Before I left the college to continue my travels through India, one of the students agreed to come with me and serve as an interpreter. He was a great help. Together we explored many states and met many people. The ministry that would soon become Reaching Indians Ministries International and Mission India was beginning to grow from an idea into a blueprint—a blueprint God was etching on my heart and mind.

Interestingly, for six months my devotions had been in the book of Nehemiah. I began to see many similarities in Nehemiah's ministry and the ministry God was calling me to. When confronted with the physical and spiritual condition of his people, Nehemiah lamented, *"When I heard these things, I sat down and wept. For some days I mourned and fasted and prayed before the God of heaven. Then I said: 'O LORD, God of heaven, the great and awesome God, who keeps his covenant of love with those who love him and obey his commands, let your ear be attentive and your eyes open to hear the prayer your servant is praying before you day and night for your servants, the people of Israel. I confess the sins we Israelites, including myself and my father's house, have committed against you. We have acted very wickedly toward you. We have not obeyed the commands, decrees and laws you gave your servant Moses'"* (Nehemiah 1:4-7).

Like Nehemiah's burden for his people, my burden for South Asia was great. As I studied Nehemiah and explored India, I wept tears for my country and her people. God opened my eyes to two realities: spiritual darkness and poverty. I saw the educated and the uneducated alike worshiping idols and ringing bells to wake up unknown gods. It was heartbreaking to see the nation held in bondage by spiritual darkness! The second harsh reality that confronted me in India was the poverty that met my eyes wherever I looked. Once, while on the train, a poor, skinny, half-naked boy came to clean my compartment. He continually scratched my leg and pleaded, "Sir, please help me." God used his hopelessness to convict me then and there—to make a difference in one person's life is an eternal accomplishment! RIMI's vision to provide for the children of South Asia grew out of my encounter with that boy and his need for the God he did not yet know.

God opened countless doors for me to meet with many different Christians, especially pastors. They continually reminded me of both the spiritual and physical needs of South Asia. God showed me the importance of raising up grassroots level church planters, evangelists, teachers, medical personnel, and social workers—providing them with both a strong biblical foundation for ministry and practical vocational training.

As I traveled, I gave to others and they gave to me. When I was admitted to the hospital with malaria, I saw the Church in action. Believers stepped in and cared for me in my time of need. God also used me to minister to others. As I traveled, I preached, taught, encouraged, and ministered wherever I went. Many people came to know the Lord. God gave us hearts full of compassion for each other.

Many times God reminded me that His ways are not my ways. Being from southern India, I had never considered launching the ministry in northern or central India. However, when I visited northern India, God opened my eyes to the poverty and spiritual darkness there. Had God not shown me these things, I would never have considered ministering there.

Soon it was May and time to return to the States. As my plane took off and I watched India fall away, I reflected on all I'd learned during my journey of discovery. I recalled the many ways God spoke to me during those months. I remembered all the sights, sounds, and feelings I had experienced. I thanked God for the friends I had made. But mostly, I grieved over the masses of people I encountered who were lost without Jesus. The faces of the poor were permanently etched into my heart. I prayed, "Lord, I am available, I will do what you want me to do."

Moni will relate the story of our joyful reunion in Chicago and the "year of two births":

"Saji returned from his six month exploratory tour of India in May, 1993. He returned with the vision of the birthing a new ministry called, Reaching Indians Ministries International (RIMI). As Mother's Day came, I realized that God had answered my prayer from the year before. It was almost overwhelming. I had prayed for God to make me a mother and now a child was growing inside me!

When Saji returned, we moved into a two bedroom apartment in Wheeling, Illinois. We call that time, "the year of two births." The first birth was of our daughter, Maryann Esther. She arrived early Saturday morning, July 31, 1993. RIMI was born the next month in our tiny apartment.

The name, "Maryann," is a combination of her grandmothers' names. Before I gave birth, Saji and I chose not to find out the sex of the baby. We wanted to be surprised. We were prepared with two different names—if a boy, Andrew; if a girl, Andrea. When our daughter was born, however, we decided to combine my mother's name, 'Mary' and Saji's mother's name, 'Ann.'

Even so, God timing is perfect! We need to trust Him.

As I look back on those months preceding our 'two births,' God's merciful hand of providence is clear to me. He ministered to us through the generosity of others. People encouraged and strengthened us during difficult times. God guarded my health throughout my pregnancy—I worked until the very day I went into labor. In fact, except for the sickness I had in India, my pregnancy was trouble-free. I enjoyed working and was grateful to be able to continue with my job. Although I wasn't making much money, the insurance covered all our medical expenses—another provision from God!

God is so faithful. I believe He has a time for everything. We don't always see what He's doing when we're in the middle of it. But afterwards, we can look back and see how God was working and understand the wisdom of His timing. When we were first longing for a baby, Saji was in school and I was working full time. We now see what a difficult time that would have been to have a child. Even so, God timing is perfect! We need to trust Him."

12

ORGANIZING THE VISION

Think big, but start small…

~ John Maxwell

After my travels throughout India, I came back to America with a better understanding of what God was calling us to do. Moni and I set out to follow the plans He had revealed. I summarized everything I saw, heard, and learned while in India into twelve observations. These observations compelled us to adopt a holistic approach to the ministry.

The first task was to share the vision with those around me. Up to that point I had primarily shared my vision and testimony with family and friends—asking them to join me in praying for South Asia. The time had come to broaden this circle of prayer warriors. One of the first people I talked to was our pastor, Jerry

The room ignited with energy as I shared and they joined in. The table before us was covered with information—notes, charts, graphs, and maps.

Foote, at the Evangelical Free Church in Wheeling, Illinois. I shared my vision with Jerry and sought his leadership and guidance. We gathered ten other people together on a warm August morning in 1993, met in the church basement and discussed how to make the vision come to life. Those present agreed to be the first board members and I began to share everything on my heart—my ideas, my experiences in journeying through India, and my burden to make a difference by organizing a large-scale effort to reach all South Asia for Christ. The room ignited with energy as I shared and they joined in. The table before us was covered with information—notes, charts, graphs, and maps.

I shared the twelve observations that had crystallized in my mind during my travels. I also shared my conviction that a holistic approach to ministry would be necessary to effectively respond to the overwhelming needs and spiritual darkness of South Asia. My twelve observations were:

1. Indigenous missions work is effective and growing rapidly.

2. Many of the Church leaders working cross-culturally in the North come from South India.

3. Some of the strongest Christian leaders in India have no formal theological training and are self-taught.

4. Most of the missionary work presently being done in India is among the lower class, or Dalits.

5. There is not enough work being done to reach the middle and upper classes for Christ.

6. There is not enough intentional and strategic planning focused on reaching each of the distinct people groups living in South Asia.

7. There is not enough grass-roots level training equipping believers to plant churches and reach villages.

—

8. Christian workers with advanced degrees are hesitant to live and minister in villages.

9. In South Asia, people everywhere are receptive to the Gospel.

10. There are not enough committed Christian leaders willing to invest their lives in difficult regions.

11. Much of the missionary work being done in South Asia is financially dependent on Western believers and organizations. In too many cases, indigenous ministries have no long-range plan for become financially self-supporting.

12. Women are very effective in life-style evangelism. They need to be empowered, motivated, and trained.

With great passion, I also spoke of an event that had occurred a hundred years earlier. On September 11, 1893, a famous Indian Guru, Swami Vivekananda, visited Chicago and addressed seven thousand delegates from all over the world at the Parliament of Religions Convention. He set out to introduce America to Hinduism. Harnessing the power of his notoriety, he captivated his listeners. He began, "Sisters and brothers of America..." However, his opening sentence was interrupted when the audience erupted with inexplicable excitement and a standing ovation. The clapping lasted more than three minutes! I shared with the new board my hope and prayer for this ministry was to stir up the same kind of fervor for mobilizing the Global Church to reach the East, and beyond, with the truth—the Truth about Christ!

The ministry's name would be important. Our name would communicate our purpose and our goals. As I shared, we became united in the vision God had given us. Because there are twenty-five million South Asians scattered throughout the world, in addition to the more than one billion living on the Indian subcontinent, we decided to give the ministry a far-reaching name. After deliberating for three hours we decided on the name *Reaching Indians Ministries International (RIMI)*.

RIMI began humbly. Our office was located in one of the bedrooms of our apartment. In the beginning our focus was promoting the vision. I worked as a school bus driver during the week while Moni continued to work at Trinity. On weekends, we traveled and shared about the immense physical and spiritual needs of South Asia. It wasn't always easy, but we persevered with the Lord's help. I remember sitting in the school bus one morning at 5 a.m. Greatly discouraged, I prayed, "Lord, did I misinterpret your call?" However, He continually reassured me that I had not. He would work everything out in His time. Once, by faith, I left for the southern United States with only one-hundred dollars, no itinerary, and few connections. My only transportation was my old car.

> **I remember sitting in the school bus one morning at 5 a.m. Greatly discouraged, I prayed, "Lord, did I misinterpret your call?"**

Like Abraham, I simply obeyed the leading of the Holy Spirit. During that trip, God showed me both the layout of America and the willingness of the believers to join God's work. I was privileged to share my testimony and vision with many groups, and recruit more partners.

In April, 1994, I also spent two months in Nagpur, Central India. There, I gathered together a group of committed leaders and founded Mission India (MI). I carefully selected ten key leaders I had met during my travels the previous year. Enduring sweltering temperatures, more than 120 degrees Fahrenheit, we met in a Nagpur hotel and established an Indian board of directors—a counterpart to RIMI's board in the

United States. Next, I rented an office building and identified an administrative leader, Abraham Mathew. Having served many years—and in many places—with the Indian government, Abraham had strong administrative skills and an understanding of Indian cultural diversity. He also spoke some of the many native languages found in India. He assumed the responsibility of managing Mission India's Nagpur office. Together Abraham and I surveyed the district of Nagpur. It consisted of fourteen counties and 1,650 villages. We made detailed plans to reach the entire district and asked God for a great harvest.

Soon after, the first church planting couple, Saji Phillip and his wife joined MI and began their ministry in Kalmeshwar County near Nagpur. As the year progressed, many more church planters and evangelists were placed by Mission India in strategic locations.

In America, RIMI also began to grow rapidly. In 1995, we rented a small office for four-hundred dollars per month. We had started a newsletter almost as soon as we started the ministry. But up to this point, we had no computer. I wrote the newsletter by hand and made multiple copies to send to our supporters. After two years, God blessed us with a used computer. We also held banquets every fall to update RIMI supporters and invite others to join the vision. The first banquets were held at our church in Wheeling, Illinois.

> **From the beginning, RIMI's strategy has centered on evangelism and saturation church planting.**

However, as the ministry grew, we needed to find a bigger place to hold our banquets. Arlington Heights Evangelical Free Church met this need. This is just one example of how God moved people and churches to advance His Kingdom through generous giving—and there were many more! At one banquet, a Christian brother who is passionate about missions, gave us enough money to buy our first Jeep for the ministry in Nagpur. We used this vehicle to move church planters and their belongings into their fields of ministry. We also transported believers to nearby rivers for baptisms. God met another need through a generous gift given in 2000. Imogene Glasmeyer, from Colorado, donated $20,000 and requested that it be used for a down payment for a house for Moni, Maryann and me. The board designated an additional $20,000 to be used toward the purchase of the house in RIMI's name. The home, located in Round Lake Beach, Illinois, would house both our family and the RIMI office.

From the beginning, RIMI's strategy has centered on evangelism and saturation church planting. As a result of God's provision and the generosity of believers, the ministry grew. Moving forward, we were able to expand and implement more of the vision God gave us by adding Mercy Homes and compassion ministries—providing food, clothing, and spiritual growth to South Asians who live impoverished and broken lives.

13

GOD'S PROVISION FOR THE VISION

"God's providence is not blind, but full of eyes."
~ *John Greenleaf Whittier*

I cannot say enough about God's provision! He took care of us and continues to do so. While we tried to get the ministry off the ground, Moni worked outside the home, providing us with an income and insurance. Eventually, I asked her to leave her job and step out with me in faith that God would support us. I needed her help in the ministry and wanted her to join the RIMI staff. In addition, Maryann, a toddler, would benefit by having her home. It was a challenge for Moni. She was legitimately concerned about the loss of a regular income and insurance. Then, during the month she was weighing the decision, a friend sent Moni a check for two-thousand dollars, her normal monthly salary. We saw this as a confirmation that God wanted her to accept a larger role in RIMI and that He would continue to provide for our needs. The Lord encouraged Moni through her friend's act of love.

God continued to take care of our financial needs. One time I went to the office and discovered an envelope under the door. Inside was two-thousand dollars in cash, which was the exact amount we needed that month for the ministry in South Asia. At Christmas time, several money gifts arrived which provided for special needs.

However, God's provisions were not always financial. Sometimes He provided people with special gifts to serve. Shortly after we moved into our first, one-room office in Wheeling, Moni and I began praying for a secretary. The ministry was growing so rapidly, we couldn't keep up with the administrative work. One day while driving, Moni and I decided to stop by a friend's house. There we met Jackie Leahy, who was also visiting them that day. We were sharing the vision of RIMI with him when our need for a secretary became known. Jackie volunteered and began helping us in the ministry. She remained with us until we moved the office from Wheeling to Round Lake Beach.

> **No longer was RIMI about my God-given hopes, my God-given dreams, and my God-given desires. RIMI was now about our God-given dreams, our God-given goals, and our God-given desires!**

Shortly after we moved to Round Lake Beach, God again met our need for administrative help. I was attending a meeting for the local pastors in northeastern Illinois. The meetings were arranged by Pastor Tom Curry. As I shared the purpose of RIMI with the group, one of the pastors, Sid Miller, asked me if I had any needs they could pray for. Hearing of our need for an administrator, Pastor Miller recommended Richard Smithers—a man in his congregation who had recently lost his job. Soon after, Richard began working for RIMI and has since become a full-time member of our ministry team. Just as God provided Richard, He continues to raise up men and women to minister with and through RIMI.

As RIMI grew, the vision God gave me became a vision shared by many others. RIMI and its supporters became the family of Christ ministering with brothers and sisters on the other side of the world. No longer was RIMI about *my* God-given hopes, *my* God-given dreams, and *my* God-given desires. RIMI was now about *our* God-given dreams, *our* God-given goals, and *our* God-given desires! I am blessed by God to be surrounded by people who see the needs of South Asia and are not afraid to act. Together—no matter what our individual roles may be—we are involved in something bigger than ourselves. In this realm of missions, only God knows what will happen. And so we obey Him, knowing if we trust and depend on Him, doors will open and all Creation will know He is God!

PART IV
MOVING OUT IN ACTION

Missions in the 21ˢᵗ Century

Pastors getting ready to be deployed into the villages

Baptism service at our Seminary Campus

One of the early RIMI house churches

14

ONE VILLAGE AT A TIME

"I will not leave Burma, until the cross is planted here forever."
~ Adoniram Judson

One of the exciting developments of the late twentieth century was the exploding growth of churches in the world. Despite challenges from secularism and sometimes fierce persecution from individuals and governments, churches worldwide continued to grow. Between 1900 and 1970, the number of Christians in Asia rose from just over 20 million to a remarkable 96 million! After 1970, Church growth exploded. By 2000, the Church had grown to over 300 million people. Growth continued to an estimated 344 million by 2005. By 2025, it is estimated that there will be one-half billion Christians on earth.

Because of the effectiveness of the indigenous movement, churches will continue to thrive in Latin America, Africa, and Asia in spite of economic and political limitations. Every day God is calling more and more native Christian workers into the mission fields of their own countries and beyond.

The Mandate

Evangelism and church planting was the heartbeat of the early Church. Acts 2 tells of Peter evangelizing the people, sharing the Gospel message, and leading them into discipling relationships and the fellowship of house churches.

It is important to note the number one priority of the local church has never been to simply gather believers together. Rather, the mandate is to *make disciples* by introducing Christ, teaching his message systematically and thoroughly, baptizing those who accept Christ personally, and nurturing ongoing growth so that people will understand and obey everything Christ taught. The purpose of teaching believers is to help them obey Christ. Obedience, not information, transforms our hearts. We make disciples in a local church setting by God's grace and in His strength. Too often leaders compete to build Christ's Church using man-made methods and programs. Apart from God, these attempts are futile and powerless. Jesus declares, *"...apart from me you can do nothing"* (John 15:5).

A key distinctive of RIMI is the strategy of planting and nurturing house churches.

The Methods

RIMI pursues the priorities of the early church: evangelism and church planting. We are not the first to implement this approach in South Asia. Reverend Thomas Matthews established Filadelfia Bible College and made a great impact in India by pursuing a philosophy of contextualized missions, establishing self-governing churches, using native workers, providing theological education, and meeting the social and physical needs of the people.

Dr. Paul Pillai also practiced these methods. He established India National Inland Mission, headquartered in New Delhi, which includes Grace Bible College, where native evangelists are trained for church planting ministry in North India. His ministry also maintains a children's home for orphans.

RIMI builds on their efforts, and of many others. Today, RIMI has over 1200 native workers evangelizing, planting churches, and serving over four-thousand house churches throughout India, as well as Nepal, Bhutan, and Sikkim.

A key distinctive of RIMI is the strategy of planting and nurturing house churches. Our training and deployment of native workers is intentional. As God opens the hearts of the local people through the teaching of His Word confirmed by miracles, new believers are trained to become strong, dynamic church members through rigorous discipleship training. Each church planter ministers in a 15-20 mile radius, establishing house churches in local villages. Because faith comes by hearing, all our church planters are passionate about sharing Christ with the lost. The Gospel is presented in many ways—telling stories to children, one-on-one personal evangelism, praying and fasting for the sick and demon possessed, visiting the sick in hospitals, revival preaching, and outreach to college and university students.

We win people to Christ by consistently sharing His genuine love. The church planter regularly visits families in the villages. He develops friendships through which he can share Christ and His love. John Ninan and A.V. Thomas drew me to Christ with their love, their committed friendship, and their regular visits.

In South Asian culture, families are closely connected and respected.

Unbelievers are initially more comfortable meeting in the home of a relative than they are in a church building. Establishing house churches also has the advantage of honoring the cultural practice of respecting elders. This has led to many coming to Christ—especially in northeast India. For instance, if a father is interested in hearing the Gospel, his whole family will listen with him. If a grandfather accepts Christ, all his children and grandchildren will be excited to join him in his new faith. Likewise, if a village leader is excited about the Gospel, his excitement will spread through the whole community and they too will likely come to faith. This cultural principle was evident when my own family came to Christ. When I—the eldest child—came to faith, it was natural for my immediate family to eventually follow suit by believing in Christ and becoming passionate about sharing Him with others.

For RIMI, planting house churches is intentional. On weekdays, church planters visit village homes, extend love and friendship, and encourage unbelievers to come to house church meetings. These meetings are often planned for weeknights because this is the time most people are home from work and other obligations. A typical house church service is between two and three hours long! There are songs, intercessory prayers, careful teaching of God's Word, discussions, and focused prayers for healing and the salvation of souls. After the service, simple meals are often shared and times of fellowship enjoyed.

Each church planter leads four or five house church meetings each week. Because it's important for every house church to grow and multiply through evangelism and discipleship, we recommend a house church grow no larger than twenty people. Eventually, each house church is managed by a mature, trained, local leader who is mentored by the full-time church planter. On Sundays, members of the various house churches in a region gather together and worship in a central location.

When a new work begins in an area, the house church meets in the church planter's rented home. Once twenty-five people trust Christ and are baptized, a piece of land is purchased, typically for about ten-thousand dollars, and a worship hall is built. Attached to the worship hall is a two to three room parsonage. The central church hall does not look like a colonial European church.

The goal of RIMI and Mission India is to plant self-supporting, self-governing churches.

Rather, it resembles a house with a large room attached to it for prayer meetings and worship services. The church planting family lives in the building and maintains it as they mentor and minister to the local house church leaders from the surrounding villages.

Every year, each local church is challenged to identify at least one person to send to the local Mission India Bible College. Church members are also challenged to support the student financially. Each candidate for Bible College is identified by the local pastor as being mature, gifted, and called. At Mission India, we are dedicated to training anyone who can read and write. Their call to ministry, however, must be confirmed by local leadership.

Pralhad Tandekar is one of the many gifted and dedicated workers we have identified, trained, and sent. Pralhad came from a poor Hindu family, and grew to know the Lord through a local church plant. He attended seminary in Nagpur and dedicated himself wholeheartedly to completing our one-year training program. When he first enrolled in seminary he did not speak English. After Pralhad completed our one-year program, he continued on and earned his Bachelor of Theology degree. During his time at Mission India Seminary, Pralhad not only mastered English—he became an excellent translator and interpreter.

Every weekend while in seminary, Pralhad went into an unreached village in a neighboring state, shared Christ, and established a local church. He baptized thirty new believers and around thirty-five people attended services each Sunday. Today, after completing an additional one year program at Tyndale Theological Seminary in Amsterdam, he is again teaching and ministering in India with RIMI. Pralhad is just one of the many examples of how God is raising up national workers to multiply His Kingdom in South Asia and beyond.

The Money

The goal of RIMI and Mission India is to plant self-supporting, self-governing churches. With this in mind, we do not offer full financial support to any of our church plants. Our desire is to provide each church plant with 50% of the financial support needed. This level of support provides partial rent and a couple meals a day for our church planters.

To provide this support, we look to missions-minded individuals and churches to partner with us. An indigenous church planter, or church planting family, can be placed in an unreached village or district for $90 - $180 per month. As global awareness grows among Christians, many believers are excited to invest in this strategic work of God. Churches in South India are excited to support the ministry of church

There will always be a need for expatriate missionaries. Even so, deploying indigenous missionaries, where possible, is much more cost-effective.

planters in North India where Christians make up less than one percent of the total population.

South Asian Christians living in other parts of the world enthusiastically support the work being done in their former homeland. South Asian Christians living in the Middle East, North America, and elsewhere are supporting thousands of Christian workers and parachurch ministries in their homelands. Many Western churches and believers also understand the importance of providing for national workers. This is demonstrated by an increase in purposeful giving through accountable indigenous missions organizations. Many Christians are recognizing the Biblical support for, and the cost effectiveness of, this model for global outreach. Beyond this, partnering with an indigenous missions agency to touch an unreached part of the world is thrilling and life-changing! Many churches and believers are experiencing this firsthand. Such partnerships provide a great opportunity for believers and churches alike to participate in a world-wide harvest of souls during the twenty-first century.

Management of Funds and Supplies

There will always be a need for expatriate missionaries. Even so, deploying indigenous missionaries, where possible, is much more cost-effective. This is why RIMI trains and deploys indigenous workers rather than expatriates. An investment of fifty-thousand to seventy-thousand dollars a year is often required to train and establish an expatriate missionary in a foreign land. Unfortunately, an expatriate worker is sometimes forced to leave the field because of political upheaval. In South Asia, the same investment of fifty to seventy thousand dollars can be used to deploy at least fifty national workers. These workers already speak the local languages, understand the local cultures, and cannot be forced out of the county. Because national workers typically minister near their family—or at least close enough to make periodic visits—discouragement is less pervasive.

Once placed, RIMI provides our missionaries with a $100 dollar bicycle and maximum support of $180 per month for a church planting family depending upon the family size and location. This support continues for six to seven years. Each year specific ministry goals are established. Support money is distributed to our church planters through their district leader. On the first Friday of every month all the church planters in a region gather at their district leader's home. They pray, fast, fellowship, report on their ministry, and receive their monthly support. Our policy is, "No report, no support!"

RIMI provides each district leader with a motorbike. This enables him to visit every church planter he supervises in all the villages where they minister at least once every month. During these visits every church planter is mentored and encouraged. The district leader also meets and ministers to church members and promotes new church planting projects in his region.

The district leader's work is monitored by his state leader and Mission India's central office. Leaders from Mission India's central office regularly visit every district to instruct, evaluate, and edify local leaders and church members.

Communication and Local Support

RIMI believes true partnership requires communication. Most Mission India district leaders have the language and computer skills necessary to communicate with sponsoring churches/individuals. This is done by e-mail, phone, newsletter, and periodic updates. Sponsoring church partners are encouraged to identify a "champion" for their RIMI project. This congregation member will consistently communicate

TRANSFORMED *for a* PURPOSE

Tear along the dotted line and mail in an envelope if including a check.

I would like to help the ministry by sponsoring:

☐ Child $30   ☐ Missionary: ☐ $30 ☐ $60 ☐ $120
☐ Bicycle $100   ☐ Motorbike $1,000

Please send me _____ more books at $12.95 (call for quantity rates)

Name _____

Address _____

City _____ State _____ Zip _____

Phone _____ Email _____

Make checks payable to RIMI

Rimi is a 501(c)(3) organization and all donations, except for books are tax deductible.
A receipt will be sent for items that qualify.

Reaching Indians
Ministries International
Church Planting, Leadership Development, Compassion

ECFA
MEMBER

15

TRAINING
TOMORROW'S LEADERS

If you can raise up leaders, you will always have followers,
but if you can't raise up leaders, you will only have followers.
~ John Maxwell

The future of missions rests in the emerging Global Church. It is essential that we invest ourselves in her—training up godly leaders empowered by the Spirit to bring her to maturity. God is doing great things in our world! He is convicting people from every tribe and tongue of their sin—and they are repenting and responding to Christ. He is revealing Himself to the hopeless through visions and miracles and convincing unbelievers that Jesus is the only Savior. Because of this, the emerging Global Church is rapidly growing in breadth!

The future of missions rests in the emerging Global Church.

Even so, it presently lacks depth. Apart from godly mentoring and systematic instruction, new Christians remain shallow. How, then, can we disciple these countless new believers who are presently responding to Christ? The answer is we cannot—not without mature, godly leadership! Without well-trained shepherds, discipling fledgling believers becomes chaotic and unproductive. Without godly national mentors, new believers remain open to deception and the Global Church remains immature.

John Maxwell, the founder of InJoy Ministries, defines leadership as "influence." RIMI's goal is to develop Biblically sound, mature national leaders to influence the local church and society at large. Such leaders must be more than overloaded information factories. Their hearts and minds must be transformed by the power of God and His Word. This is paramount! Think about the problems that presently challenge India:[1]

- 40% of the world's poor are Indians
- Three hundred million Indians have an income of less than $1 a day
- 100 million Indian families have no source of water at home
- 150 million Indian households have no electricity
- 30% of the villages in India are not connected by roads
- India is home to the world's 2nd largest HIV population

In our present generation, it is especially heartbreaking to read these statistics. Why does a four-thousand-year-old nation continue to suffer from such widespread poverty? Is it because of lack of vision or an inability to adapt to changing times? Unlikely! There are many brilliant people living in India. Unfortunately, a corrupt social system too often discourages the initiative that produces positive change. Consequently, while the middle and upper classes

Indigenous leadership—both secular and Christian—must be developed in order to promote progress and positive change.

1 India Today, Bridging the Divide, Special edition, March 27, 2006

thrive economically and technologically, the lower classes—who are barred from such opportunity—are being left behind. If someone in the political arena attempts to change the system, he or she will most likely be attacked and thwarted by the opposition. Because of the instability of coalition governments, visionary politicians have often been unable to exact permanent positive change.

What then is the answer? By God's grace and by the power of prayer, the nation can be transformed by raising up and multiplying the number of effective leaders from within. Time is of the essence! South Asia cannot wait for Western leadership to step in and turn their society in a positive direction. Indigenous leadership—both secular and Christian—must be developed in order to promote progress and positive change.

Training Mandate

"Go and make disciples." Christ gave this mandate just prior to His final ascension (Matthew 28:18-20). Making disciples for Christ is not an easy job! It is labor intensive. Fulfilling Jesus' mandate requires the same creativity and perseverance possessed by those foreign missionaries who served South Asia in the past. They toiled and suffered to bring us basic education and medical help—and to development indigenous national leaders. Today, many South Asian leaders—discipled by these dedicated expatriate missionaries—are picking up the torch and forging ahead for India.

Paul stated the purpose of his ministry in Colossians 1:28-29, *"Him we proclaim, warning every man and teaching every man in all wisdom, that we may present every man mature in Christ. For this I toil, striving with all the energy which he mightily inspires within me..."* Paul is clear. His purpose in leading was to make disciples mature in Christ. He believed and taught that all the treasures of wisdom and knowledge are hidden in Christ. Therefore, our passion must be the same—to introduce the person of Christ, to proclaim God's Word, and to help believers grow into Christ-like leaders. This is our heart and passion at RIMI! Our dream is to raise up 100,000 men and women who will lead and serve in South Asia and beyond. Like Paul, we are dreaming big and starting small—one leader at a time.

Training Methods

In the Bible, God gives His people a model for developing leaders. When we started RIMI, we planned and developed our ministry in stages. We based our strategy on the model the Lord gave us.

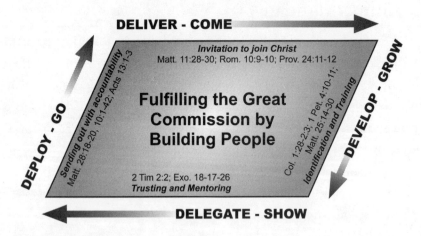

Discipleship Process Model

DELIVER - COME

DEPLOY - GO

DEVELOP - GROW

Sending out with accountability
Matt. 28:18-20; 10:1-42; Acts 13:1-3

Invitation to join Christ
Matt. 11:28-30; Rom. 10:9-10; Prov. 24:11-12

Fulfilling the Great Commission by Building People

Col. 1:28-2:3; 1 Pet. 4:10-11;
Matt. 25:14-30
Identification and Training

2 Tim 2:2; Exo. 18-17-26
Trusting and Mentoring

DELEGATE - SHOW

Stage One: Deliverance

Deliverance of the unsaved person from spiritual darkness and oppression is accomplished by presenting the Gospel of Christ clearly. Christ invites everyone who is weary to come unto Him. Jesus said,

"Come to me, all who labor and are heavy laden, and I will give you rest. Take my yoke upon you, and learn from me; for I am gentle and lowly in heart, and you will find rest for your souls. For my yoke is easy, and my burden is light" (Matthew 11: 28-29).

The many "yokes" of this world oppress people. For many years, my family was oppressed by deception and satanic attack. Many members of my extended family still have not humbled themselves and accepted Christ as their personal Savior and

> **Contextualization means presenting Christ in the language and context of the people we are trying to reach.**

Lord. They continue to suffer and live without real hope and peace. They are missing out on God's wonderful plan for their lives. How tragic!

In order to deliver people from darkness, we must meet them where they are. Whenever possible, we must identify with our hearers in their lifestyle and communicate the Truth in the way they can best comprehend it. This is called contextualization. Contextualization means presenting Christ in the language and context of the people we are trying to reach. It means using terminology they understand so they can better comprehend the Good News of Christ. This is why RIMI deploys trained national missionaries to live among those we hunger to reach for Christ. As a part of their community, Mission India church-planters lovingly, relevantly, and consistently share the message of Christ. But how can they be sent without the support of a sender? Both the indigenous missionary and the one who sends him/her are critical to what God is doing in India through RIMI. Together, both missionary and sender can rejoice in the harvest.

In this generation, God's Spirit is working powerfully! Everywhere people are seeking and searching for the Truth. They are finding meaning and purpose in Christ. My friend, Ravi Narasimhan, a former Brahmin, searched long and hard for "Truth." He finally discovered his purpose while reading the Gospel of John. He accepted Christ. Today, he is a leader at Motorola in Chicago. He actively shares the hope he found in Christ by word and deed.

Spiritual hunger is especially evident among the youth of India—50% of India's population is under 25! For them, lasting hope can only be found in Christ. For example, two young men from Orissa came to our seminary in Nagpur to learn more about Christ. When they discovered the Truth, they gave their lives to Jesus. In Him, they found meaning and purpose. During that year, both were baptized and continued to grow in their faith. One is now a theological student in Amsterdam. The other is pursuing an advanced degree in theology at an Indian Bible college. These young men, and others like them, impassion my heart and life! They remind me of the way Christ saved me at the age of twenty and how I, in turn, shared Jesus with every member of my family. I saw God's saving grace spread through my village and beyond. Young people are the future of any nation. That is why RIMI actively reaches out to them. When God opens the heart of a young person, He also opens a door for us to help them develop their talents and gifts for Christ's glory.

Unfortunately, many talents remain hidden and unused because they go unrecognized.

Stage Two: Development

Every believer who comes into one of our local churches brings his/her God-given gifts into the Body of Christ. Each has an impact on the Kingdom of God because of His endowment of creativity. It is the role of local leadership to identify and help develop the gifts of every believer in the church—whether a child, a youth, or an adult. Unfortunately, many talents remain hidden and unused because they go unrecognized.

Growing up, few people recognized or helped me develop the gifts God gave me. It was not until I cultivated friendships with fellow believers in America that my gifts came to light. One positive attribute possessed by the American Church is this—when a believer has a good idea, he/she is encouraged to pursue it. In the same way, when a believer has a gift or talent, he/she is encouraged to use it—regardless of the person's background. In America, believers are given opportunities to use their gifts and work out their ideas for the glory of God. Not only did my American friends recognize my gifts and calling, they gave me opportunities to develop them. They encouraged me and held me accountable to progress in learning.

This is an example for the South Asian Church to follow. RIMI and Mission India are committed to identifying and developing the gifts and potential of every believer in the local church—especially among the "untouchables" and other poor classes where encouragement is rarely practiced.

My friend, Pastor Joseph Raju, lives in Delhi. He is a powerful example of how God uses people from all backgrounds—developing their gifts for use in His Kingdom. Raju grew up in an orphanage and did not enjoy the love of a father. He was angry and rebellious. By God's grace, Raju was saved. He did not have good grades in high school and did not speak English well. Even so, because of his persistence and determination, he was ultimately admitted to a local Bible College. To everyone's surprise, Raju graduated with distinction. He became one of the best preachers in his graduating class. Today, after completing a degree in theology, he is the academic dean of a Bible College and pastor of an Assembly of God congregation in Delhi.

Pastor Joseph Raju's example should encourage us to help our Christian brothers and sisters identify and utilize their God-given gifts for the advancement of Christ's Kingdom. One of RIMI's core values is that building up people always takes priority over building up programs. Rather than see each other for what we are, we must learn to see each other for what

> **Outside of a mentoring relationship, developing leaders often becomes performance-driven and begins to ignore the importance of character development and growth towards Christ-likeness.**

we can become in Christ. This will cause us to pray for one another and spur each other on to become everything God intends us to be.

Stage Three: Delegation

As RIMI helps believers discover their gifts, we strive to involve them in specific ministries where those gifts can be utilized. As they minister, and continue to be mentored, they grow in their confidence that Christ can abundantly use them in His kingdom work. Without proper mentoring, many young leaders suffer setbacks and discouragement. Outside of a mentoring relationship, developing leaders often become performance-driven and begin to ignore the importance of character development and growth towards Christ-likeness. This is why RIMI is committed to training leaders through mentoring relationships with those more mature in their faith and more experienced in ministry.

Delegation is the key for the multiplication of leaders. When the burden of ministry became too great for Moses, Jethro advised his son-in-law to delegate (Exodus 18:17-26). Likewise, Paul told Timothy to entrust the task of discipleship to other capable leaders (2 Timothy 2:2). RIMI strives to delegate tasks by clearly defining responsibilities and lines of authority. Without clear expectations, leaders can become weak and confused in their tasks. It's unfortunate, but many ministries are exclusively led by one family—or by a single charismatic director. They expect their workers to do nothing more than follow instructions. Very little, if any, leadership development, mentoring, or peer leadership takes place within these ministries. Over time, these ministries experience a disappointing decrease of effectiveness and influence.

One reason RIMI has grown so rapidly in South Asia, is our commitment to identify ordinary people full of potential to do great things for God. We love them, share our vision with them, mentor them—and then release them into their field of ministry with clearly defined tasks. In this, we give our leaders both time and freedom to shine through the exercise of their God-given gifts. This principle of delegation results in greater productivity on the field.

Stage Four: Deployment

Deployment is the "going" stage of ministry! Having been mentored and trained, young leaders are offered new ministry opportunities—opportunities beyond the scope of their current service. This may or may not involve moving to another region in their state. These ministry opportunities are tailored according to each worker's experience, maturity, and giftedness. Deployment is not abandonment! We do not send leaders out to minister alone. We offer guidance and support. We regularly monitor progress and offer our missionaries encouragement along the way. The ministry of RIMI is intentionally structured to provide on going management training and oversight at every level.

When a local church is unable to support the training of a new leader from its congregation, RIMI helps by providing full or partial scholarships. Our long-term goal is to see every local Mission India church deploy and support at least one person each year for leadership training and church planting.

RIMI has developed eight leadership programs designed to equip and deploy national workers:

- Mission India Bible Colleges
- Mission India Theological Seminary
- Summer Bible schools
- Short-term seminars and conferences
- Mission India Family Conference
- Job skill training
- International conferences and networks
- Selective training in overseas ministry

Mission India Bible Colleges

India has twenty-eight states, eighteen major languages, and many dialects. RIMI strives to train native missionary workers within the context and culture of the place they'll be serving. Today (2008), RIMI has a local Bible college in twenty-three Indian states. Our vision is to build at least one school in every state. Every RIMI Bible College is born in humble circumstances. Typically, a Bible College starts with ten to fifteen students and meets in a rented house. A fully established college can train up to one hundred students. A RIMI Bible college is administered by a capable, experienced, well-educated state coordinator who is passionate about church planting. He is usually from the state where the Bible College is located and understands its culture and language. About half of the college's courses are taught by the state coordinator. Other classes are taught by experienced church planters. Each Bible College serves as a discipleship center. Faculty/student relationships are strong. This reflects the Biblical model for leadership development. Jesus taught His disciples by spending time with them. He did not just tell them how to do ministry, He showed them.

The RIMI Bible College training program runs for three semesters. It focuses on discipleship and church planting. On weekends, the students get hands-on experience by ministering with local pastors in evangelizing, teaching Sunday school, and conducting church services. Upon completion of the one year program, students receive a diploma in Theology and Church Planting.

Coursework at our Bible Colleges are taught in the local language of each host state. This presents a challenge because study Bibles, commentaries, and textbooks are seldom available in these languages. RIMI's vision is to develop or acquire these ministry tools in the future.

The cost of financing a RIMI Bible College, training twenty-five students, is $2500 per month. This sum covers rent, salaries, classroom supplies, and the cost of feeding and housing the students.

Our ultimate goal is for each Bible College to own its own building on a two or three acre campus. It currently cost around $300,000 to buy property and build a facility that can house fifty students, a Mercy Home for fifty local orphans/needy children, a technical training center, a medical clinic, a library, classrooms and faculty apartments.

Mission India Theological Seminary (MITS)

In 1994 I asked God to show me a thirty acre piece of land in or around Nagpur—the geographic center of India. We prayed about and visited many locations. We did not wait for land, however, to start Mission India Theological Seminary (MITS).

Beginning in 1995, MITS began operation in a small office building. Our students slept in the same room where classes were held. Those students were humble and hungry to study God's Word. They were unhindered by the cramped and uncomfortable conditions. We offered a one-year program. Many of our classes were taught by field workers. This enabled our students to learn practical lessons from our missionaries along with the truths of God's Word. As we ministered in this way, God revealed our need for a permanent campus.

In 1999, we found a thirty acre piece of land about ten kilometers northwest of the Mission India main office in Wadi. Although it was surrounded by Hindu families—which typically hinders Christian land purchases—God opened doors and we purchased the land in 2000. We held a ground-breaking ceremony and began construction by faith. We only had $5000 in hand. Before and during the entire construction process, many people prayed and fasted. God was faithful. As we built, the funds came in—always on time!

God also forged critical partnerships with key believers to complete the task. Good friends, Robert and Jan Schill, from Phoenix, Arizona, sacrificially committed themselves to planning the campus. Bob, a respected architect, traveled with me to Nagpur to design the campus. He studied the land and developed a master plan for building one of the finest theological seminaries in South Asia.

Mission India Theological Seminary is open to students from various evangelical backgrounds. Scholarships are available for eligible students. We especially welcome students from North India where the Gospel has not yet penetrated. Our goal is to train and graduate dynamic leaders who will shape the world by planting churches in South Asia and beyond. We prepare students to face challenges and seize the opportunities God gives them.

In addition to theological training, the seminary will soon train students in medicine, nursing, farming, basic job skills, and management. By providing technical training such as computer science, electrical work, carpentry, auto mechanics, air conditioning maintenance/repair, toy making and more—we want to empower local believers to escape poverty and become financially independent. In addition, a 100-bed hospital is currently being built on-campus to serve the surrounding community.

Sixty to seventy percent of our graduating students are currently being deployed in church planting ministries.

MITS is presently moving towards full accreditation. It will ultimately offer a variety of theological degrees including Bachelor of Theology, Master of Divinity, Master of Theology, and doctoral programs. The seminary is managed by quality leaders who represent many of the people groups that populate South Asia.

Presently, half of the MITS campus has been built. We currently have the capacity to train 350-400 students each year. As our technical training building nears completion, we have forged ahead and instituted training programs in computers, toy making, screen printing, and other skills. Our library is operating and is one of the finest in all of South Asia. New books are continuously being added as the Lord provides. Our hospital and nursing schools are not yet open, but a fully functioning on-campus clinic provides medical care for the surrounding community.

Sixty to seventy percent of our graduating students are currently being deployed in church planting ministries. Other graduates pursue additional studies or return to serve in their home churches. We continue to look to the Lord for His timely and miraculous provision of the remaining three million dollars needed to complete a campus that will ultimately house and train 1000 students a year!

Summer Bible Schools

RIMI's Summer Bible Schools offer forty-day, intensive training programs for Christian high school students and other interested believers. Bible training sessions are offered every year from March 20 to May 30, between college and seminary sessions when our campuses are unoccupied. Training sessions focus on developing godly character and evangelism skills. Graduates of our summer Bible schools return home and minister in their local churches. Later, some will attend the seminary or one of our Bible colleges and prepare for full-time ministry.

The training RIMI offers through Mission India Theological Seminary and our twenty-three Bible colleges prepares more than 1000 young leaders a year for ministry. The cost of training is about $60 per month per student.

Short-Term Seminars and Conferences

In addition to the leadership training provided through our seminary and Bible colleges, RIMI offers well-planned seminars and conferences throughout South Asia. These seminars, taught in many languages, typically last from one day to a week. In most cases, they are free to participants. Our training conferences offer our missionaries the opportunity to leave their villages and network with other pastors and church planters. Together they pray, learn, and encounter new ideas and ministry methods. We invite experienced leaders from South Asia and beyond to lead these seminars. In 2006, Tim Inman, my friend and RIMI board member, and I visited many cities in North India. We taught and encouraged over one-thousand indigenous leaders. RIMI strives to send church leaders back to their villages with renewed enthusiasm and fresh approaches for effective ministry. These seminars are provided to our missionaries for an approximate cost of $25 per person (per day) for food, housing, travel, and materials.

Mission India Family Conference

The Mission India Family Conference is a national annual event that gathers, encourages, and empowers all of our workers and leaders. The conference provides an opportunity to network, fellowship, and bond as a spiritual family. It is an exciting time of testimony, and provides an opportunity to set ministry goals for the next year. Every state's ministry goals are discussed and factored into RIMI's overall ministry goals. This meeting helps us know how to budget and pray during the coming year. The Family Conference is a rich time of encouragement and accountability.

The Mission India Family Conference usually takes place in the month of October during the Diwali Festival, when most South Asians have a two-week holiday. The organizing team carefully selects a conference theme each year. In 2006 we studied 1 Corinthians using the theme, "Changing Asia by Living for Christ." About 1000 leaders come from all over South Asia. Some traveled for three days to get to Nagpur—and another three days back home. We strive to invite the best teachers from South Asia and America to teach God's Word. The Mission India Family Conference is a special time for our leaders to come together for a week and be taught by great men and women of God. Although it is a huge commitment for RIMI to pay for each worker to attend the conference, we feel it is of utmost importance to honor them, encourage them, and cover their expenses. This annual conference costs us about fifty-thousand dollars—or about fifty dollars per attendee.

Job Skill Training

South Asia has multitudes of people who need to be trained in basic job skills. Most of India's poor cannot afford the educational and vocational training programs offered by private corporations or businesses. Therefore, RIMI endeavors to provide basic job skill training to each Bible college student. This enables each missionary to provide some of their own support as their church-plant grows. Our program is currently affiliated with the local government polytechnic school. Students are taught various skills, including computer skills, toy making, screen printing, electrical training, plumbing, carpentry, and auto mechanics. Since our job skills courses are affiliated with a government school, our graduates receive government-approved certificates. RIMI's goal is to expand our course offerings by networking with professionals in the West who can teach courses or invest financially in our job skill training programs.

International Conferences and Networks

In addition to offering indigenous church leaders training opportunities within India, RIMI also sends qualified leaders to international training conferences. Enabling our South Asian ministry leaders to experience other cultures and network with other world-class leaders is vital to RIMI's future. Currently, we send some of our key leaders to the Haggai Conference in Singapore. Many of our leaders travel throughout Asia, since it is affordable and easy to get visas. We also send selected leaders to international conferences held in South Asia. International conferences provide networking opportunities that enable us to meet the leaders of other Pan-Asian ministries and learn from them. Recently some of our leaders attended the *Vision 20/20 Conference* in Chennai. They heard powerful testimonies of God's work in Asia and were encouraged and motivated.

Higher Education in International Schools

One of RIMI's dreams is to develop world-class Christian leaders by sending key leaders to study at world renowned theological schools. There they can specialize in critical areas of study under world-class teachers. In June 2007, Rajesh Sebastian, graduated from Dallas Theological Seminary. This opportunity was made possible thanks to our partnership with Stonebriar Community Church in Frisco, Texas.

All of these special leadership programs: Mission India Bible Colleges, Mission India Theological Seminary, summer Bible schools, short-term seminars & conferences, the Mission India Family Conference, job skill training, international conferences & networks, and training key leaders at world-renowned seminaries, are integral to RIMI's overall strategy of raising up multitudes of leaders to reach

South Asia for Christ. We are launching and nurturing each of these ministries as the Lord provides and the mission grows.

16

CALLED TO COMPASSION

The King will reply, "I tell you the truth, whatever you did for
one of the least of these brothers of mine, you did for me."

~ *Matthew 25:40*

"Compassion is the empathetic pity that wants to spare, relieve, or nurture somebody who is suffering."[2] God is gracious and compassionate, and since we are made in His image, we are endowed with similar attributes. In Him, we are creatures of compassion.

God's compassion is seen throughout the Bible. In spite of their pride and rejection of Him, He dealt with the people of Israel compassionately. He heard their cries and continuously delivered them from crushing oppression and the rivalry of their enemies.

In the New Testament, Christ demonstrated His compassion during his public ministry (Matthew 9:35-36). Jesus glorified the Father through His power and compassion when He healed multitudes of people plagued by disease.

The Apostle Paul commands us to act accordingly. As God's children, we must offer compassionate service to those in need. He

2 Cornelius Plantinga, Jr, Contours of Christian Compassion, Perspectives V.10 page 9

writes, *"Be kind and compassionate to one another, forgiving each other, just as in Christ God forgave you"* (Eph 4:32). Paul exhorts us again in Colossians 3:12, *"As God's chosen people, clothe yourselves with compassion, kindness, humility, gentleness, and patience."*

Those who love God and righteously follow Him must demonstrate compassion to those around them in word and deed. To act otherwise undermines one's testimony of commitment to Jesus Christ. We are Christ's light in a dark world—a world full of problems and poverty. We are *"the salt of the earth, and if the salt loses its saltiness, then it is useless"* (Matthew 5:13). Comforting words without compassionate actions are worthless!

RIMI is committed to reaching out to the people of South Asia with the genuine love of God. Believers who involve themselves in innovative projects that alleviate the problems and pain of suffering people are living examples of what it means to be "salt and light." Every person can do something to make a difference in this world by showing compassion. Sometimes, however, the problems seem so overwhelming, we are tempted to think we can do nothing at all.

> **We may think our labor is small and ineffective, but if motivated by a heart of compassion, even our smallest acts are meaningful. Showing compassion "to the least of these" is obedience to Christ.**

A common story is told of a boy who showed compassion on starfish that had washed up on the shore. Knowing they would die, he decided to throw them back into the sea—one by one. A man walking by noticed the boy's effort. He scolded the boy and told him he was wasting his time. There were just too many starfish. What difference could he make? Ignoring the man's comments, the boy picked up another starfish and threw it back into the water. "Sir," he said, "I made a difference for that one."

We may think our labor is small and ineffective, but if motivated by a heart of compassion, even our smallest acts are meaningful. Showing compassion "to the least of these" is obedience to Christ. We can all make an eternal difference in someone's life—one person at a time!

RIMI's Compassion Ministries

RIMI strives to demonstrate Christ's love in South Asia and beyond through a number of compassion ministries. As in the story of the starfish, the needs of South Asia are overwhelming. About three-hundred million Indian people, equal to the population of the U.S., currently live in deep poverty. This staggering number is almost beyond comprehension! God has mercifully filled my heart with deep compassion for those who are poor and suffering. While growing up in India I encountered needy people daily. In my own life, I faced many hardships—scarcity of food, clothing, money, and more. As I got to know the person of Jesus Christ, His compassion became real to me. I came to see how important it is for RIMI to step out in faith and make compassion a priority. Compassion has become an integral part of our vision to reach South Asia. We continually seek practical and creative ways, often despite our lack of funds and manpower, to meet the physical and material needs of people as we share the Gospel with them.

One of RIMI's vital and dynamic compassion ministries is making a difference for children. Our vision is to establish two Mercy Homes for children in every Indian state and beyond. Each of these homes will house 100 children. Today, RIMI has 22 Mercy Homes for boys and girls, supporting over six-hundred children. The children who live in our Mercy Homes are cared for by a qualified family or care-taker. They are most often identified and invited to live in a Mercy Home by our field workers. Some of the children are orphans, but not many. Because of South Asia's pervasive poverty, many parents are unable to support their own children. They are sent to various homes, both secular and Christian, throughout South Asia. Unfortunately, many of these homes do not offer proper care. RIMI is committed to providing reputable Mercy Homes that offer the best care—safeguarding the welfare of the children and preparing them for productive futures.

RIMI Mercy Homes house children of all ages. They stay with us until they complete their education. Our goal is to raise up tomorrow's Christ-like leaders for both the ministry and the marketplace. Because of this, we strive to send the children to local private schools where they can get the best education. If such schools are not available, the children attend a public school.

Every day our Mercy Home children participate in devotions and worship—both in the morning and evening. Most of the children accept Christ within one or two months of their arrival. They regularly sing songs and memorize Bible verses. Every Sunday there are opportunities for them to share their testimonies. In addition, they memorize one verse from the Bible during the worship service. They are daily encouraged and motivated to grow in Christ!

In addition to Children's Mercy Homes, we also have a "Helping Hands" program that supports children whose Christian parents are poor. When parents are committed Christians and able to raise their children well, we encourage them to keep their children in their family home. RIMI then helps support the family with food and provision for their children's education. Every year, we have thousands of requests for help. Typically a child in the "Helping Hands" program can be sponsored for thirty dollars per month. For three-thousand dollars per month, a Mercy Home of one-hundred children can be sponsored.

Another compassion ministry offered by RIMI is our medical awareness camps. With the help of qualified volunteers, we offer medical check-ups and teach villagers ways to improve their lifestyles—such as AIDS awareness, sanitation, and early childhood development. Sometimes 250-500 needy villagers show up for medical camp! Medical camps give us opportunities to introduce Christ to the participants in a non-threatening environment. Many times hearts and minds are changed—not by arguing—but by acts of caring.

Another pressing need God is calling RIMI to respond to is the spread of HIV and AIDS. India has the second largest HIV population in the world. Often, because of India's caste system and parochialism, HIV infected people are outcasts. Even their own families reject them! Many in South Asia are ignorant about issues related to HIV. This is in spite of government efforts to raise HIV awareness through the national and local media.

Because of ignorance, fear, and perceived medical risk, building an HIV ministry is a challenge. It is difficult to build a program, find a facility, and recruit people for this kind of ministry. Pray that God will provide wisdom and funding as we seek to share the love of Christ with people infected with HIV.

17

INDIGENOUS OWNERSHIP

And you Philippians yourselves know that in the beginning of the gospel, when I left Macedonia, no church entered into partnership with me in giving and receiving except you only.

~ Philippians 4:15

The American Heritage Dictionary defines "ownership" as "that which belongs to one." This defines the RIMI perspective on ministry. It is imperative for South Asian believers to take *ownership* in ministry. RIMI's goal is to establish self-supporting, self-governing, and self-propagating indigenous churches in South Asia and among South Asians worldwide. This is a critical concept that South Asia and the Global Church must grasp. For centuries, the mindset and methods of missions and evangelism has been dominated by colonialism. Foreign workers raised and received full financial support from home while living and ministering among nationals. The South Asian Church grew to depend on the outside funding that came from the sending agencies of foreign workers. Typically, these foreign workers did not help national believers and churches become autonomous by teaching them to support and govern themselves. When these foreign workers retired and returned to their native countries, indigenous church leaders struggled and the national church found it difficult to stand on its own.

Unfortunately, this historically Western model still impacts many national believers today. Rather than take leadership, many indigenous workers still consider themselves employees of their supporting missions agencies. As such, they expect continual financial support from these agencies. This weak and unhealthy mindset is unbiblical and debilitating. The purpose of a biblically functioning missions agency is to jump-start the work of evangelism and church planting. As they minister, church leaders must prepare nationals to take ownership of the Lord's work by teaching every believer the importance of serving and giving in obedience to Christ's teaching. This is part of true discipleship and is the key to church growth and sustainability.

> **RIMI's goal is to establish self-supporting, self-governing, and self-propagating indigenous churches in South Asia and among South Asians worldwide.**

RIMI is intentionally structured to train nationals to take ownership in ministry. Our staff is carefully selected and called to be change-agents. We have developed a model for ministry that is more effective than the historical colonial model. We begin by encouraging church planters to help support their families by working part-time as they minister and establish their churches. Sometimes, this approach is not appreciated by our church planters. This is due to the old cultural understanding of what is expected of ministers. Traditionally, local priests come from the upper caste and involve themselves only in temple activities. Lower castes are not permitted to perform temple rituals. This same mentality has crept into the Christian church where the notion remains that a pastor should not work outside of ministry. This results in false expectations. First, the church planter may believe—based on history and tradition—that as a mission agency "employee," he or she can expect to thrive financially. Other church planters assume the opposite—they expect to live in severe poverty. Both expectations are driven by cultural and personal pride. Embracing either demonstrates a lack of understanding. The Bible pictures the early church growing under leaders who combined secular work with their Christian service.

Jesus was a carpenter. Paul was a tent-maker. He was satisfied to work and supplement his income. He set an example and challenged the Ephesian elders with these words, *"I coveted no one's silver or gold or apparel. You yourselves know that these hands ministered to my necessities, and to those who were with me. In all things I have shown you that by so toiling one must help the weak, remembering the words of the Lord Jesus, how he said, 'It is more blessed to give than to receive'"* (Acts 20:33-35).

RIMI encourages each national pastor to take ownership of his ministry. This includes supporting himself. Field workers are also encouraged to develop leadership within their churches to help administer and implement effective ministry in their local context. In this way, every believer is encouraged to be involved in, and take ownership of, the ministry of his or her local church. Additionally, every church plant is affiliated with our national organization, Mission India. This affiliation is important for spiritual accountability, for responding to various government regulations, and for collective planning on a national level. RIMI is not about establishing another denomination. Rather, our desire to create a Biblical movement that establishes and supports many organizations and leaders.

God provides in His way and according to His timetable. Even without on-going Western support, many churches and organizations are thriving in South Asia. My friend, John Ninan, started evangelistic work in my home village after completing his Bible college training. His church's central office only provided for his rent. He trusted God for his food and all other expenses. John established a dynamic church in the village and, according to God's design, the "Body" sacrificially supported him and the work.

One member of John's church, George, worked hard selling vegetables and black pepper to support his family and the church. George struggled with his health and died young. Even so, he is a true hero of the faith who did not waste his life. He was one among the many national believers who lived, and still live, their lives by faith without a fear of suffering.

> **RIMI is not about establishing another denomination. Rather, our desire to create a biblical movement that establishes and supports many organizations and leaders.**

George obeyed God by working and giving generously to advance God's Kingdom. During his short life, the simple village church John Ninan planted—and George supported—raised up, discipled, and deployed seven church planting leaders!

Saji Thomas and his wife Sherly also exemplify what it means for indigenous pastors to take ownership in their ministries. Saji is from Southern India and Sherly grew up in Northern India. Sherly is fluent in three languages. She used her gifts to establish and run an English grade school in their village in order to subsidize the church planting work of her husband. Today, the local church is self-supporting and offers scholarships to the students they send to the Mission India Bible College.

At RIMI, we are convinced that promoting national ownership of our South Asian ministry is a fundamental part of our calling. The value of local ownership in ministry is instilled in our workers and practiced on the field. Even so, national ownership of ministry on a local level does not mean independence from the Global Church. We cannot reach South Asia alone. RIMI's ministry depends on its partnership with the Western Church. We seek short-term financial and mentoring partnerships that help our pastors plant churches that ultimately become self-supporting. Through these partnerships, new church plants are given start-up funds. Typically, the level of support is reduced each year until and, usually around the fifth year, the church becomes fully self-supporting.

Because of the economic situation and per capita income of most local believers, we seek global partners willing to invest, not only in new churches, but also Bible College buildings, special projects, annual operating budgets, and modest salaries for our pastors. These start-up funds provide a foundation for ministry local believers can build on. In time, these ministries will not only become self-sufficient—they will, in turn, invest in other new ministries even as others invested in them.

18

STEWARDSHIP–OUR CALLING

Moreover it is required in stewards that one be found faithful.

~ I Corinthians 4:2

Jesus talked a great deal about money in the Bible. Sixteen of his thirty-eight parables related to handling money and possessions. In the Gospels, one out of every ten verses directly deals with the subject of money. The Bible offers five-hundred verses on prayer, less than five-hundred verses on faith, and more than two-thousand verses on money and possessions. God makes it clear—the way we view and handle money is critical to our Christian lives! Following are some Biblical principles that offer God's perspective on how we are to think about and invest money (Adopted from Generous Giving website):

1. **God Owns Everything, and I Am His Money Manager**

    • Psalms 24:1 *"The earth is the Lord's, and everything in it, the world, and all who live in it."*

2. **My Heart Always Goes Where I Put God's Money**

    • Ecclesiastes 5:12 *"The sleep of a laborer is sweet, whether he eats little or much, but the abundance of a rich man permits him no sleep."*

- Proverbs 18:10-11 *"The name of the LORD is a strong tower; the righteous run to it and are safe. The wealth of the rich is their fortified city; they imagine it an unscalable wall."*

- Matthew 6:19-21 *"Do not store up for yourselves treasures on earth, where moth and rust destroy, and where thieves break in and steal. But store up for yourselves treasures in heaven, where moth and rust do not destroy, and where thieves do not break in and steal. For where your treasure is, there your heart will be also."*

3. This Present World Is Not My Permanent Home

- Philippians 3:20 *"But our citizenship is in heaven..."*

- Luke 12:15 *"Then he said to them, 'Watch out! Be on your guard against all kinds of greed; a man's life does not consist in the abundance of his possessions.'"*

4. I Should Not Live Merely for the Moment but for Eternity

- Hebrews 11:25-26 *"[Moses] chose to be mistreated along with the people of God rather than to enjoy the pleasures of sin for a short time. He regarded disgrace for the sake of Christ as of greater value than the treasures of Egypt, because he was looking ahead to his reward."*

- Matthew 25:21 *"His master replied, 'Well done, good and faithful servant! You have been faithful with a few things; I will put you in charge of many things. Come and share your master's happiness!'"*

5. Giving Is the Only Antidote to Materialism

- Ecclesiastes 5:10, 13-14 *"Whoever loves money never has money enough; whoever loves wealth is never satisfied with his income. This too is meaningless ... I have seen a grievous evil under the sun:*

wealth hoarded to the harm of its owner, or wealth lost through some misfortune, so that when he has a son there is nothing left for him."

- Mark 10:21 *"Jesus looked at him and loved him. 'One thing you lack,' he said. 'Go, sell everything you have and give to the poor, and you will have treasure in heaven. Then come, follow me.' "*

6. God Prospers Me to Raise not Only my Standard of Living, but my Standard of Giving

- 2 Corinthians 9:10-13 *"Now he who supplies seed to the sower and bread for food will also supply and increase your store of seed and will enlarge the harvest of your righteousness. You will be made rich in every way so that you can be generous on every occasion, and through us your generosity will result in thanksgiving to God. This service that you perform is not only supplying the needs of God's people but is also overflowing in many expressions of thanks to God. Because of the service by which you have proved yourselves, men will praise God for the obedience that accompanies your confession of the gospel of Christ, and for your generosity in sharing with them and with everyone else."*

- Luke 12:33 *"Sell your possessions and give to the poor. Provide purses for yourselves that will not wear out, a treasure in heaven that will not be exhausted, where no thief comes near and no moth destroys."*

- Acts 20:35 *"It is more blessed to give than to receive..."*

The Reality of Giving in America

It is my opinion America has risen to its level of global strength and power because of its founding fathers' commitment to Almighty

God. God has enabled America to be at the forefront of education, productivity, and prosperity so it can bless the world. America is also a great nation because of the generosity of its people. Many committed Christians give generously to honor God and partner in world evangelism.

Globally, Christians are compassionate in helping the poor. Many believers sacrificially give to help less fortunate nations. When I was growing up, my village school benefited from the generosity of others. I received free lunches because of help given by the American government. Today, thousands of pastors, seminaries, Bible colleges, and many compassion ministries operating around the world are supported financially through the generosity of the Global Church.

Why God Blesses Us

God does not bless us so we can be selfish and arrogant with our possessions. King David said, *"God be merciful to us and bless us, and cause his face to shine upon us. That your way may be known on earth, your salvation among all nations"* (Psalms 67:1-2). God has blessed us so that the nations of the world can know and worship Him.

Jesus disciples were, and are, commanded, *"But you will receive power when the Holy Spirit comes on you; and you will be my witnesses in Jerusalem, and in all Judea and Samaria, and to the ends of the earth"* (Acts 1:8). We are to tell others about Jesus in our neighborhoods—branching out from there as He empowers us. In America and South Asia, the immediate needs of our local churches and communities often overwhelm us. As we try to faithfully minister and make an impact in people's lives locally, it's easy to become "near-sighted" and overlook broader needs that exist beyond our line-of-sight. Learning to minister to those outside of our own "Jerusalem" requires maturity and discipline. As we grow in faith, the Holy Spirit prompts us to think more globally so we can serve and evangelize new and unreached places.

Westerners tend to respond more fully to God's charge to evangelize the world and fund global ministry than do young South Asian believers and leaders. This is due to America's strong educational system, a deeper understanding of God's Word, and more available wealth. Yet, in terms of how Christ's command to "go make disciples of all nations" is practically obeyed, the similarities between

God does not bless us so that we can be selfish and arrogant with our possessions.

Western and Eastern Christians are remarkable. Most giving in the South Asian Church, and for that matter in the Global Church, remains with the local congregation. Giving designated for world missions typically accounts for only a small percentage of a church's total giving.

Fortunately, in some churches, God has moved in the hearts of believers, who respond by giving generously to the cause of global outreach. Even so, some current surveys indicate that less than 1% of U.S. giving is allocated to missions outside of America. The average Western Christian gives only one penny a day to global missions![3]

In light of this, I believe God is calling more Western Christians to boldly devote themselves to His global cause. Those who answer God's call will be required to reorder their priorities and adjust their lifestyles with eternity in view. And those who respond? They will know the joy of partnering with believers in other nations to win lost souls and shine God's light in dark places.

---

3 Yohannan, K.P, *Revolution in World Missions*, Page 191

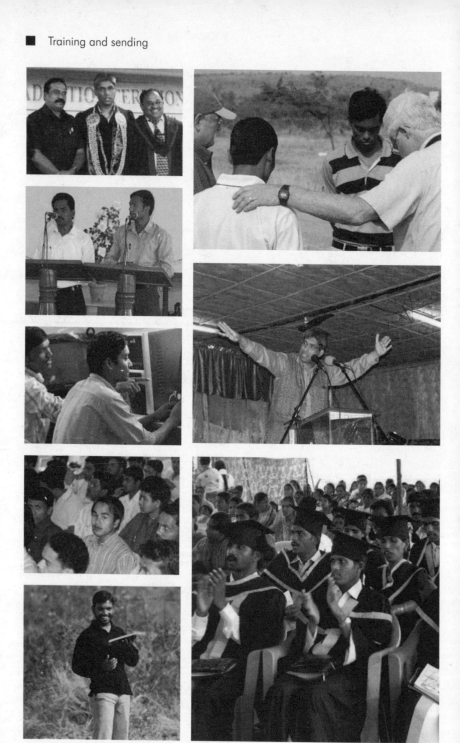

19

PARTNERING WITH THE GLOBAL CHURCH

Global church partnership is powerful and pervasive.
It's like a marriage—creating new life, but committed to an
exciting life-long relationship. As the genuine body of Christ
we are not independent but interdependent.

~ Saji Lukos

As the Western Church struggles with the day to day demands of contemporary culture, spiritual growth and vitality can suffer. Believers are often lost in the same meaningless maze for survival as unbelievers. Christians easily lose their first love like the believers in Ephesus (Revelation 2:4-6). Without real passion for God and His purposes how can the Western Church be zealous for the ministry of their local church, let alone world missions? One key to maintaining our zeal for God is recognizing that both the local church and individual believers can make a difference for God in missions. We can bring the Gospel to unreached peoples by intentionally and strategically resisting the status quo! Embrace this truth and many barriers that hinder our wholehearted response to the Great Commission will fall. So where do we begin? Here are some principles and ideas for you and your church family to consider:

Diligently resisting distractions is essential to effective participation in God's global cause. Church leaders are continuously confronted with the immediate needs of their own congregations, denominations, and communities. Their focus is naturally drawn to these pressing needs of the moment—needs they can see with their eyes and touch with their hands. Thus, it's easy for unseen global needs to take a back seat to such obvious and immediate issues. A church leader might even be tempted to think his or her local church is unable to participate in God's Great Commission—taking Christ to the uttermost parts of the world. After all, his or her own local community is desperately lost as well. These perceptions are, of course, not true!

At RIMI, we have seen how a pastor's passion for world missions impacts a congregation. When a pastor becomes passionate about global ministry, his excitement is infectious. When a pastor reminds the congregation of Christ's call to proclaim Him "to the ends of the earth," his own obedience to that call lends credibility and authority to his preaching. When a pastor is burdened for the world, he proactively promotes missions within the church. He establishes and empowers a missions committee/ministry team. He makes prayer for the global church, the persecuted church, and individual missionaries a priority in congregational life. He boldly reminds the Body of "God's economy"—encouraging believers to store up heavenly treasures for themselves by funding global outreach. In all of this, a pastor becomes an instrument the Holy Spirit uses to ignite a church's passion for reaching those imprisoned by spiritual darkness.

The same principle works on the campus as well. When the president of a Christian college or seminary catches a vision for world missions—and lends his or her voice to the cause—both faculty members and students catch the vision too.

Unfortunately, the opposite is also true! When a leader's voice is silent concerning the spiritual need of the nations an attitude of apathy generally prevails in the church and on the campus towards those living in darkness. When a leader refuses to promote global ministry, global ministry will usually not be promoted at all. God's question, "Whom shall I send?" will only be answered by silence. Church and parachurch leaders can make or break the cause of world missions.

Religious and political conflicts are bringing the un-reached to America's doorstep. Hatred towards western countries, especially the United States, is on the rise in the Middle East and elsewhere. The paradox is that many people who live in

In all this, a pastor becomes an instrument the Holy Spirit uses to ignite a church's passion for reaching those imprisoned by spiritual darkness.

these countries want to immigrate to the West! Over 100,000 students are coming from India every year to study in American universities. Many of these students attempt to stay in the U.S. because of the opportunities America provides.

Many Christian churches in America, and the West in general, recognize these immigration trends to be an exciting opportunity to reach unbelievers. Cities, suburbs, and rural towns have become home to unreached, immigrant neighbors, many who live next door to Christians. Befriending these guests, sharing the Gospel with them— and sending them back to share Christ in their homelands—may be one of the most efficient and cost effective ways to fulfill the Great Commission. Many Western churches are sharing Christ and His love with immigrants by teaching English, tutoring, and hosting foreign students. Once foreign students or workers come to Christ and are discipled, the church can support their return to their homelands. There, they can minister in places where Western missionaries cannot go. This is just one example of how churches serious about reaching the world for Christ are becoming creative in their approach to world missions.

God calls us to simplify our lifestyles for the sake of others. A story is told about a father and his two sons. The father was poor. Even so, he worked hard as a day laborer for the sake of

---

We must choose for ourselves where our allegiance lies.

---

his children. He sacrificially supported his sons and provided them with good educations. The oldest son got a good job and moved to Dubai. He lived well. The younger son worked as a school teacher and a farmer and remained close to home. Even though he struggled financially, he worked hard to provide for his five children and support his now widowed father.

When their father grew old, weak, and sick, the younger brother asked his older brother to come home for a few months so he could help care for their father. The older brother always found excuses not to come. He forgot how his father had suffered and worked to give him an education and the prosperity he now enjoyed. He also failed to appreciate the sacrifices his younger brother had made to provide for his father in his waning years. In the midst of his prosperous and busy life in Dubai, the older son became ungrateful. He lost sight of the debt he owed to his family!

The older son's attitude angered his younger brother. Even so, he continued to care for his beloved father. In spite of their poverty, his five children also poured out their lives caring for their grandpa. One day the poor younger brother went to his dad's bedroom. He said,

"Dad, I love you. You have given me life. As long as I have strength in me, I will take care of you." His father was filled with emotion. He cried and thanked his son in a low, weak voice.

While this story is especially poignant in South Asian culture, I think Christians everywhere should see it as a metaphor relating to our attitude towards God. Do we truly appreciate the debt we owe our Lord and Savior? In Romans 1:14-15 Paul understood his obligation, *"I am obligated both to Greeks and non-Greeks, both the wise and the foolish. That is why I am so eager to preach the gospel also to you who are at Rome."*

Are we committed to Him and to the work of His Kingdom? It does not matter how much money we make. It does not matter where we live. It does

We must be passionate like the early Christians in their zeal to reach the lost.

not matter whether those around us are generous or stingy. We must choose for ourselves where our allegiance lies. We must choose for ourselves whether or not we will generously support God's Kingdom work with the time and resources we have. Each of us can make room in our lives and in our budgets to help others come to know Christ personally. We can individually choose to take an active role in honoring our commitment to fulfill the Great Commission.

Sending is as valid as going. Some people think, "I just can't become a church planter," or, "The Lord hasn't called me to go to the mission field." Others say, "Since I can't or won't go, I'll give some money instead. Maybe God will be satisfied with that." In the end, however, whether we "go" or "send" is not as important to God as the condition of our heart. Whether we go or send, we must all personally invest ourselves in God's global cause. As followers of Christ, we are all responsible for reaching the lost. In Scripture, God commands each of us to do our part in fulfilling the Great Commission. As each of us individually pursue God's will for our lives, those called to send joyfully partner with those called to go—and Christ is proclaimed in places where He has never been known before. The world has yet to see the miraculous outcomes that await our prayerful and unified obedience as we work together to reach the lost!

Christ's final mandate to his disciples was to "go into all the world and preach the Gospel, making disciples of every nation" (Matthew 28:18-20). One of our top priorities in the church should be obeying this call to take Christ to "the ends of the earth." This begins where we live. Every day we need to reach out to family members, co-workers, and neighbors and share the good news of Christ. We must be passionate like the early Christians in their zeal to reach the lost! Even though the early Christians lived in the midst of persecution, we are told, *"Among them, daily the Lord added those who were being saved"* (Acts 2:47). Our witness at home is an integral part of what God is doing around the world to bring others to Himself. Beyond this, we must each relish God's plan for our involvement in world missions—whether we are called to "go" or to "send." We must be enthusiastic and proud partners in God's global cause!

Seven Steps for Promoting World Missions

Because six thousand unreached people groups remain in the world today, we must energetically teach and promote missions in the local church. Why? Because the local church is God's chosen instrument for evangelizing the world. All of the human and financial resources for reaching the lost lay within her. I offer seven suggestions for promoting missions in the local church. These suggestions can be summed up in three core values, presented in the following figure:

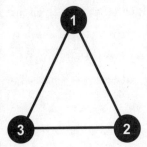

1. **A clear vision with a statement**
2. **Well-defined strategies and programs**
3. **Strong leadership**

1. Belief in Biblical Foundations

The foundation of Christian missions comes from the Bible alone. The Bible is clear—our God is a missionary God! At the moment of humanity's first sin God promised to send a Savior (Genesis 3:15). God's covenant with Abraham is a missionary covenant in which He promises to bless "all peoples on earth" (Genesis 12:3). Israel was called by God to be a missionary nation (Psalm 67). And, in the incarnation, God Himself became the greatest missionary of all—*"In the beginning was the Word, and the Word was with God, and the Word was God. ...The Word became flesh and lived for a while among us. We have seen his glory, the glory of the one and only Son, who came from the Father, full of grace and truth"* (John 1:1, 14). Is it any wonder that our missionary God calls us to be missionaries too? *"All authority in heaven and on earth has been given to me. Therefore, go and make disciples of all nations..."* (Matthew 28:18-19). *"But you will receive power when the Holy Spirit comes on you; and you will be my witnesses in Jerusalem, and in Judea and Samaria, and to the ends of the earth"* (Acts 1:8).

In his book, *Understanding Christian Missions*, Herbert J. Kane summarizes the Biblical foundation of missions, "It is part of God's sovereignty in the realm of redemption. From the first to last the

Christian mission is God's mission, not man's. It originated in the heart of God. It is based on the love of God. It is determined by the will of God. Its mandate was enunciated by the Son of God. Its rationale is explained in the Word of God. For its ultimate success it is dependent on the power of God."

In his book, *Missions in the 21st Century,* Tom Telford adds, "Missions is on every page of the Bible. It starts in Genesis and is wrapped up in Revelation, when the whole world will be worshipping Jesus."[4]

Sadly, today, many church-goers question the authority of God's Word—and thus our missionary obligation. Many have been influenced by our pluralistic society in which the very idea of absolute truth is rejected. Others disregard the authority of Scripture because it inconveniences them—threatening their personal agendas. Many who profess Christ are, at the same time, striving to become rich in the things of this world. This causes them to ignore their Biblical responsibility to practice godly stewardship and generosity. What a tragedy! If we profess Christ and believe the Bible is true, we must boldly believe and apply its teachings to our personal lives. And one thing is certain—the Bible teaches missions!

Not only must we understand and believe in the Biblical foundations for missions, we must have bold leadership in the local church to implement and lead world missions.

2. Strong Missions Leadership

Leadership plays a crucial role in mobilizing a local church for global ministry. Under the Spirit's influence, believers respond to strong, Biblical teaching that flows from a heart passionate about

---

4 *Missions in the 21st Century* by Tom Telford with Lois Shaw, Page 143.

world evangelism. That is why it is important for the senior leadership of a church—especially the preaching pastor—to regularly teach on missions. If the senior pastor is not excited about missions, usually God's people will not be either.

In his book, *The Church Is Bigger Than You Think*, Patrick Johnson observes, "Many pastors of busy churches are so overwhelmed by the pressures and needs of their own congregation and local challenges, that there seems no time for what is only going to create more work--promoting

> **If we profess Christ and believe the Bible is true, we must boldly believe and apply its teachings to our personal lives.**

missions. It may take the same combination of sufferings and delegation of authority in modern congregations to provoke obedience to the Great Commission."[5]

One church that understands the priority of the Great Commission is Elmbrook Church in Waukesha, WI. Because of the influence of Stuart and Jill Briscoe, Elmbrook is a great missions church. Their growing missions budget, presently over 1 ½ million dollars annually, supports over 130 workers. Elmbrook Church is impacting the world for Christ!

But a church does not have to be large to make an impact in God's global cause. Intermountain Baptist Church in Salt Lake City, a church with an average attendance of 100, partners with RIMI. The families of this church support ten Indian church planters, partially support our Bible College in Gujarat, and have raised funds to purchase land for a Bible College and Mercy Home campus.

God never intended a believer's involvement in His global cause to

---

5 Patrick Johnstone, *The Church is Bigger than You Think*, Page 46.

be sporadic or reactionary. By His design, our commitment to missions should be an ongoing and long-term commitment. Whether we live in a small American town, a city in Zimbabwe, or a suburb of Tokyo, we are all called to do our part to fulfill the Great Commission. We have ethnic groups dwelling with us in our own communities. In Chicago alone, newspapers are published in more than 100 different languages. We live in a diverse, busy world, populated with lost people who need to hear the Gospel. If we do not share with them, who will?

Pastors must constantly remind believers of the Church's mandate (Matthew 28:18-20). We must share with the hurting people of our communities from the heart of Jesus. Congregations must be made aware of the plight of the lost through testimonies and good preaching that will move the hearts of God's people. We see this happening in South Asia where most of our churches take time during worship services for testimonies to be shared by members of the congregation. These testimonies encourage and strengthen believers. They also greatly impact visitors who come from other faiths.

Awareness of our world's spiritual need can also be raised by regularly sharing relevant statistics and showing good missions videos. These reminders of what God is doing in other parts of the world are a powerful way to maintain a church's involvement in God's global cause. Encouraging church members to read missionary biographies and other missions books also helps maintain a focus on the Great Commission and how God wants to use each of us to fulfill it. On a congregational level, fulfilling the Great Commission is enhanced by developing a strong vision statement for global missions.

3. Strong Vision and a Working Missions Statement

"Without vision, people perish" (Proverbs 29:18a). Mobilizing the Global Church at the local level requires clear vision and committed leadership. John Maxwell reminds us, "Everything rises and falls on the basis of leadership." Because of this, a mature, Biblically sound, dynamic leader ought to be chosen to lead the church's missions ministry. If the church

> **Ideally, missions committee members will be "missions-minded" people and not simply people who have extra time but no passion for the lost.**

is large and financially sound, it is wise to hire a full-time staff member to lead the missions program—working along with a capable missions board or committee. This person must be called by God. He/she must love people, have a passion for lost souls, and possess gifts of teaching and administration/organization. If the church is small, the missions ministry is best lead by someone with these same gifts—supported by the pastor and a carefully selected missions committee/board. Members of the missions committee must be knowledgeable and passionate about their ministry. A well-defined missions policy should be established in order to avoid confusion and keep the church's mission vision focused. This is important because the committee's membership will likely change from year to year.

Sometimes, I am disappointed when I present RIMI's ministry to missions committees or boards. In some churches, committee members have trouble relating to our vision. At times, they seem bored with the work and/or ask outdated or irrelevant questions. Some committees seem unaware of how God is working in the world today. In these churches, God calls me to patiently and prayerfully reach out and help them understand what is happening today in His global church. I try to ignite their own sense of calling as missions leaders and renew their passion for the work. I offer ideas about how to mobilize their church family to participate in what God is doing around the world. Ideally, missions committee members will be "missions-minded" people and not simply people who have extra time but no passion for the lost. If possible, committee members should be representative of the Global Church by including believers from different national and ethnic backgrounds. These volunteers should be discipled in the area of missions and learn from committee members from other churches are already making a global impact for Christ.

A missions committee's effectiveness is, in part, dependent upon a well-crafted missions statement. A good missions statement enables the committee to focus and prioritize the church's global ministry. A good missions statement is rooted in the vision and philosophy of the church and its leadership. The statement will be both urgent and relevant. It should reflect the changing times, for example what God is doing around the world today. Without an awareness of the current needs around us, how can we make a difference? How do we prioritize the needs and maximize the funds?

The Lausanne Conference held in Thailand in 2004, noted some of the major changes taking place in the world today. These changes call us to rethink and re-strategize our approach to missions:

"The dramatic change in the political and economic landscape in recent years has raised new challenges in evangelization for the church. The polarization between east and west makes it imperative that the church seek God's direction for the appropriate responses to the present challenges. In the 31 Issue Groups

these new realities were taken into consideration, including the HIV pandemic, terrorism, globalization, the global role of media, poverty, persecution of Christians, fragmented families, political and religious nationalism, post-modern mind set, oppression of children, urbanization, neglect of the disabled and others".[6]

In order to develop relevant local and global missions ministries, leadership must consider such realities as they craft their own church's missions statement. Following is the missions statement of College Church in Wheaton, Illinois:

The Missions at College Church shall be defined as ministry which fulfills the Great Commission by proclaiming the Gospel of Jesus Christ cross-culturally through evangelism. Discipleship, Bible translation, church planting and church leadership development, giving priority to the unreached. We recognize the importance of meeting physical needs and educational needs when this serves the growth of the gospel. The Board of Missions helps College Church reach people with the gospel beyond our culture and thus fulfill God's mission to bring glory to himself by redeeming a nucleus of believers from every distinct language and cultural group on earth.[7]

Here are some challenging questions to ask ourselves and our churches: Do we have a current missions statement for our church? What kind of leadership have we appointed to oversee our missions ministry? Have we defined our global vision? Does our written missions statement adequately define our commitment to God's global cause, our strategy to make a difference in that cause, and our funding priorities? Have we identified capable people within the congregation to implement the vision?

---

6 Lausanne Occasional Paper (LOP) No. 39, 2004 Forum for World Evangelization held in Thailand. This Issue Group on this topic was Issue Group No. 10 (there were 31 Issue Groups at the Forum) Series Editor for the 2004 Forum Occasional Papers (commencing with LOP 30):

7 College Church website www.college-church.org

4. Casting the Vision

Once a dynamic missions statement has been crafted, it must be effectively communicated to the church. It should be done in such a way that everyone from the church, both children and adults, members and nonmembers, will catch the vision for missions. Everyone who sets foot in the church should know the church is actively involved in missions, in what areas the church is supporting missions, and how they can personally partner with the church.

There are many creative ways to cast the vision. For example, each year a church in Texas produces a powerful video presentation to share with the congregation. During that Sunday service, the senior pastor preaches on missions and the congregation

Still, God's vision is a vision of partnership that includes both indigenous workers and Western believers.

is given a detailed update of the work they support in India. Every church member is challenged to personally get involved in missions in a strategic way.

Some churches make a missions update part of the pastoral prayer for the offering. While praying for the offering, the elders pray specifically for the missionaries and their needs. Some churches put up a world map with lights or push-pins highlighting the areas where they have missionaries working. Many churches have a missions emphasis week. During this week, all church activities are centered around updating the people about the missions work and encouraging them to get involved in whatever way that they can.

5. Relevant Programs

The focus of the Global Church must be to deploy both Western and national workers in the field. I have made a strong case for the effectiveness of indigenous missions! Even so, I cannot ignore the obvious fact that the Western church must send their own sons and daughters to serve and work in foreign fields. The Bible clearly states that all churches are called to set apart members for missionary service. Led by the Holy Spirit, the church at Antioch set apart Barnabas and Paul for the work of missions (Acts 13:1-3). Our Sovereign God can—and will—call anyone at anytime to anywhere for whatever purpose He desires. We are deliberate about teaching this in the new churches we plant in South Asia. We know that as new believers mature, we must also send workers to the ends of the earth. This is our Biblical mandate.

Today's world is changing. Global concentrations of Christians are no longer found only in the West. It's exciting to think about it! Today, Korea is the second largest missions sending country in the world. For centuries, Western missionaries labored and suffered in foreign lands for Christ. On the foundation they laid, God has now raised up a powerful body of native workers all over the world. Many are now coming West to reach unbelievers from all backgrounds. For example, Pastor Sunday Adelaja, originally from Nigeria, now leads Embassy of God, the largest evangelical charismatic church in Europe in Kiev, Ukraine. The church has 20,000 members! Most are native Ukrainians.

Sending out national workers is relatively inexpensive. These missionaries are effective because they already know the languages and cultures they are ministering in. They easily adopt local standards of living and naturally identify with the people because they are one of them. Still, God's vision is a vision of partnership that includes both indigenous workers and Western believers. The Western Church is now sending qualified believers to serve, train, support, supplement, and assist national workers, even in countries that restrict missionary activity. This partnership is relevant and amazing! For example, RIMI invites experienced Greek and Hebrew teachers to India to teach at our seminary. Recently, David Whitcomb from Decatur, Alabama served for more than two months training staff in our library. We are encouraged and continue to look for more partners like David.

> **Only a small percentage of expatriate workers are directly involved in evangelism and discipleship.**

Some proven local church missions programs include:

Annual Missions Conferences: One exciting way churches can effectively convey the importance of missions and inspire people to climb on board, is by organizing at least one missions conference a year to celebrate God's work around the world. The entire local church can unite in planning the event and invite an influential speaker, preferably someone from outside the U.S. Together the speaker and congregation can rejoice in the work that God is doing through the Global Church. If planned and coordinated well, expenses can be kept to a minimum—believers can simply listen, fellowship, and share in the wondrous work God is doing in local churches all over the world. If done well, this conference will be eagerly anticipated each year and serve as the spotlight for the missions ministry of the church.

My friend, Garret Laferty told me about his experience at Elmbrook Church during their missions conference. Their missions pastor demonstrated his commitment to, and familiarity with, each of the church's missionaries. He introduced every missionary, their spouse, and their children by name from memory! The stories and pictures shared by the missionaries elevated the church's passion for missions—especially cross-cultural work.

Long-Term and Short-Term Missions: When considering global partnerships, a local church must be selective in who they "send," by partnering with credible U.S. and native missions agencies. Furthermore, the church must identify called, capable people for long and short-term missions. It is best if prospective candidates demonstrate their calling and gifting at the local church level before they endeavor to do ministry in other regions.

> **Presently, a short-term missions trips to South Asia cost about $3,000 to $3,500 per person for two weeks. For the same amount of money, a South Asian Bible student can be trained for three years.**

The candidate must gain training and experience before being sent out for long-term missions. Many workers have returned from the foreign field after only a few years because of discouragement and burn-out. For this reason, it is imperative for workers to receive the best possible pastoral care so he or she can be most effective in the field.

It is important for a local church to evaluate the various needs that exist around the world and seek God's direction concerning their specific involvement in missions. Questions to consider include: How will the church's missions funds be allocated? What types of ministries will the church support and recruit workers for? Very often Western missionaries are involved in service-based missions rather than church planting and leadership development. Only a small percentage of expatriate workers are directly involved in evangelism and discipleship. This is where the greatest need lies. Many countries are closed to Western missionaries and/or forbid Westerners from evangelizing and planting churches. In these places it is often best for American believers to invest resources, i.e. time, gifts, and money, to help develop and train national leaders so they can evangelize, plant churches, and disciple new believers.

Short-term missions trips for Western believers must be carefully planned. It is difficult for local ministers in the field to host a group of inexperienced, well-intentioned, enthusiastic guests who don't speak the local language! Expectations, goals and plans must be realistic. They must be based on what can actually be accomplished under the leadership of the local native worker.

It is important for church groups considering a short-term trip to research the details and weigh the cost of their effort while considering other options. Short-term missions trips are usually expensive—even when the group goes to a nearby city or state. Presently, a short-term missions trips to South Asia cost about $3,000 to $3,500 per person for two weeks. For the same amount of money, a South Asian Bible student can be trained for three years!

It is also important to remember that complications sometimes occur when a group of Western Christians come to places like South Asia for a short-term missions trip. Therefore, an attitude of humility and a willingness to serve is a necessity. A short-term missionary's top priority should be learning from national believers and encouraging them in their leadership rather than finding fault, scrutinizing their work or creating dependency. Often, national workers have many pressing personal needs. They tend to ask for help from their Western guests. Responding to these requests with unauthorized gifts can create jealousy among other national workers. Such support also bypasses national leadership and creates administrative head-aches.

None of these cautions are intended to discourage participation in short-term mission trips. God greatly uses such trips—especially in the life of the sending church.

Missions-Based Projects: There are many specific needs on the mission field. By contacting local leadership or the mission agency you are working with, a Western church can find out what specific needs a native missionary or church plant has. Because so many needs exist, it is important for a church to review its missions goals before diving in. RIMI offers a variety of missions projects that the entire church can be involved in. Each project is important and cost-effective. These projects include Mercy Home support ($30 per child), sending Bibles ($2 per Bible),

> **Whatever the method or tradition might be, I suggest that the church designate thirty percent of its budget for world missions.**

supporting a national pastoral couple ($120 per month), providing bicycles for church-planters ($110 per bicycle), providing motorbikes for district leaders ($1200 per motorbike), and/or providing a church hall with a parsonage ($10,000 per church hall).

There are numerous projects sponsored by many missions organizations around the world. A little research results in a great number of opportunities. Why not get involved today?

Individual Involvement of Church Members: Some church leaders are very possessive of their members' money and discourage individuals from getting directly involved with any missions project not directly related to their church. This is unfortunate! Instead, church leaders should encourage every believer to get involved in whatever missions opportunity is close to his or her heart. A pastor once told me that their budget was full and that the church was not interested in supporting any additional missionaries or missions projects. However, he was open-minded. He invited me to share my testimony and RIMI's vision with his congregation. The church was encouraged and challenged. Today many of his church members independently support a Bible school in North India.

As churches establish relationships with leaders and pastors in the field, senior pastors and/or members of the supporting church should plan a visit to South Asia. Such a trip is a "vacation with a purpose." It not only encourages church members—it strengthens the relationship between the church and the indigenous pastor in the field. These are just a few of the opportunities that exist for you and your church to be a part of global missions.

> **God blessed Moni and me when we began to step out in faith by meeting the needs of others beyond our capability.**

6. Faith Promise

Churches adopt many different methods for funding missions. These methods are typically rooted in church tradition or the preferences of church leaders. Whatever the method or tradition might be, I suggest the church designate thirty percent of its budget for world missions. This portion of the budget would include support for evangelism, discipleship, and compassion ministries. This commitment to finance ministry to the "uttermost parts of the earth" reveals a local church's heart for missions.

One specific method for funding missions is to ask believers to make a Faith Promise. A Faith Promise is a commitment made to God to give a certain amount of money weekly, monthly, or annually—over and above the regular tithe—as an act of faith and obedience to help fulfill the Great Commission. This Biblically based method for supporting global ministry was introduced a century ago by A. B. Simpson, founder of the Christian and Missionary Alliance. He based Faith Promise on 2 Corinthians 8:1-2, where we are told that the Macedonian believers gave "beyond their ability."

I have personally adopted the practice of making Faith Promises. This practice continually challenges me to live by faith and trust in God's provision. Our faith grows and our joy is multiplied when we see firsthand the ways God enables us to meet our Faith Promise. God blessed Moni and I when we began to step out in faith by meeting the needs of others beyond our capability, not only did God bless us personally, He multiplied the ministry of RIMI.

7. Mobilizing the Church to Pray

The importance of prayer to missions can never be overstated. It is vital! All genuine ministry is the work of God. Effective ministry is nothing more, or less, than God doing His work through His servants. Prayer, then, is essential to ministry. No ministry can grow or transform lives apart from prayer. Churches must teach and challenge believers to pray individually and corporately—asking God to meet needs and accomplish His will in all things. When the early church earnestly prayed for Peter, God miraculously intervened and delivered him from prison (Acts 12:5-11).

Believers should corporately and individually pray for their pastors and the many needs of the Global Church. Our pastors in India face many daily challenges in their ministries. I often receive e-mails from our South Asian leaders about church planters who are being pursued or harassed by the local authorities or religious extremists. One such leader is currently responsible for forty-two new believers who come from various faiths and backgrounds. If he is imprisoned, how will these new believers function without his leadership? Many of our pastors live in dangerous circumstances. Our prayers for their safety and protection do not go unanswered!

Missions is not an option, it is an obligation.

God also answers our prayers for provision. One time when I was in India, we did not have enough money to purchase food for our two-hundred students. I told all our staff and students to close down the entire operation for a day and come to the chapel. We gathered, worshipped, and cried out for God to intervene. We cried out to experience the God of Elijah in our lives. As the day drew to an end, we went to bed and slept. In my spirit I knew God was going to do something for us and for His glory. He did!

Even as we prayed that day, God was speaking to a man in Maine. Prompted by the Holy Spirit, he called Moni and told her he was immediately transferring stocks worth twenty-thousand dollars to RIMI's account—without knowing of our specific need and our fervent prayers. When I rose the next day, Moni called me from Chicago and shared the good news of the gift. Encouraged beyond measure, I immediately gathered our seminary students and staff together. There was such joy when I shared the news! Our God is a living God! He is faithful! He met all the needs of the school for the next two months.

Another powerful story of prayer was shared in a Lausanne paper.[8] Jong-Yun Lee serves as the pastor of Seoul Presbyterian Church,

---

8 Lausanne Occasional Paper (LOP) No. 39, page 10

which now attracts more than ten-thousand worshippers. However, the church's beginnings were humble.

Lee was a teacher in a theological seminary when he was asked in 1988 to consider a call to become the pastor of an historic congregation in Seoul. The congregation had been in a major building program for several years. Both the budget and the morale of the church were in serious decline. In fact, the enormous debt on the long awaited five-thousand seat sanctuary was staggering. It was a millstone around everyone's neck! Prayerfully, Lee accepted the call. Recognizing that he was in a position similar to Moses standing on the shore of the Red Sea, he called for a "Red Sea Strategy"— forty days of prayer and fasting, preaching from the book of Acts, and no mention of the building debt! He trusted God to provide a way where there was "no way." At first, only a handful of the congregation answered the call to pray. However, as the days and weeks passed by, the sanctuary began to fill, day and night, with praying people. At the end of forty days, a second 'forty days of prayer' began. Lee invited men, women, and children to become part of small groups that prayed around the clock. He referred to this approach as the "Jericho Strategy"—utilizing surrounding prayer to win the battle. During the second forty days of prayer, the entire debt was paid off and the church was liberated!

Now is the time to promote world missions in the local church. Missions is not an option, it is an obligation! We must obey God and return to our first love. Church leaders need a new vision, a new heart, and a new call to mobilize the Global Church to become a catalyst for reaching all peoples in our communities and around the world. We must be strategic in our missions planning and programming. We must make giving to reach the unreached a priority. We must joyfully partner with national believers in their ministries by giving, going, building relationships, and humbly assisting indigenous leaders however God leads. All this can only be done in God's power as we willingly obey Him.

PART V

MOVING AHEAD IN PARTNERSHIPS

Throughout the years, many brave men and women have answered God's call to join with me in bringing the Gospel of Jesus Christ to the land of South Asia. These are men and women who believe missions is not an option, and they prove it with their lives. I hope their stories in the following chapters will help inspire you to become an active partner in God's work around the world — especially in native missions.

~Saji K. Lukos

20

A HUNGER FOR THE TRUTH

By Pastor Richard P. Carlson
RIMI board member and Superintendent of the Intermountain
West District of the Evangelical Free Church of America

In December, 2000, I traveled from village to village in India on dry, rocky, dusty roads. Some of the local people wore homemade masks in their attempt to breathe as they walked. Spiritual warfare is the daily fare in South Asia, but the evidences of God's glory abound. I am blessed to have witnessed firsthand God's work in the hearts of those He created.

The poverty and beggars I saw broke my heart. A visit to the home of one dear RIMI pastor and his wife especially left an indelible impression on my soul. They minister to the "untouchables." As we fellowshipped in their humble home, another RIMI pastor, who ministers to unsaved lepers in a nearby colony, was dumped on the street by the officials who had imprisoned and beaten him. They persecuted him for his faith. This man is included among those described by Hebrews 11:38, *"people of whom the world was not worthy."* I went to him immediately and held him in my arms. My heart rejoiced at the opportunity to touch him, hold him, and affirm him for his faith. I witnessed firsthand how the words of the Apostle Paul apply to South Asia, *"For a wide door for effective service has opened to me, and there are many adversaries"* (I Corinthians 16:9).

God opened this door of opportunity to me! He gave me opportunity to preach, to evangelize, and to touch the hearts of beautiful people with His genuine love, humility, compassion, and passion for His Word. I shared my own life story with folks who wanted to hold and touch a person whom they knew loved them. I received Christ's courage to share His glorious love and Gospel wherever God led me and whenever He called me to speak. At the Bible Institute in Nagpur, I was privileged to be a "dad" to many of the students who begged for the opportunity to carry my attaché case and serve me as I loved them by teaching God's Word. Greater still, was the privilege I had to teach them how to evangelize their own people.

While there, I required my students to bring a friend to class, using the methods of witnesses I had taught them. They brought their friends, and I shared Christ with them. Thirty-three lost and hopeless people from the streets of Nagpur prayed to receive Jesus. I instructed the students to follow up with those who had professed Christ by using the discipleship materials I supplied. As I prepared to leave for a week, I instructed

> **At the Bible Institute in Nagpur, I was privileged to be a "dad" to many of the students who begged for the opportunity to carry my attaché case and serve me as I loved them by teaching God's Word.**

each student to use what they had learned to share Christ with the lost while I was gone. When I returned, I discovered that every student had completed this assignment. God used their faithfulness to bring sixty-six people to Jesus. The fruit of one student's effort stood out. During my absence, God used his faithfulness to bring thirty people to Christ! Even so, the memory that haunts me is of the sweet young lady seated on the aisle on the left side of the classroom. She was weeping. I couldn't bear her tears so I asked Pastor Andrew Pedron, one of my interpreters, to ask her why she was crying. She said that she had witnessed to many people but not one had prayed to receive Jesus. She felt she had failed the Lord. In this poignant moment I lifted this precious young lady up before the class. I told these twenty-eight Bible School students that if they could all have her zeal for Christ and love for the lost, the Lord would bring many more South Asians into His loving arms. I stood beside this young woman, whose heart was full of love for the lost, and prayed down God's blessing on her. I saw the light that had vanished from her eyes return.

In India I was reminded—everywhere we look, God is preparing hearts to receive Him. When we first arrived in India, I shared with an Armenian from Tehran, Iran while still at the airport. He had heard the Gospel before, but was so hungry. Willingly and joyfully, Saro Rostrami bowed to receive Jesus as his personal Savior. Earlier, while still in Minneapolis, a man named Nick Nixon received Jesus. Nick's brother, and a pastor working at the airport Burger King, had been faithfully witnessing to him before he prayed with me. Jesus tells us in John 4:38, *"I sent you to reap that for which you have not labored; others have labored; and you have entered into their labor."*

Traveling the streets of Indian cities, you see yoked oxen pulling heavy loads of cotton, dogs running freely, and cows (which are sacred) everywhere. During my time there I got used to preaching without shoes on, Indian style. As I preached barefoot, the words God spoke to Moses from the burning bush came to me, *"Remove your sandals from your feet, for the place on which you are standing is holy ground"* (Exodus 3:5).

As Saji and I traveled together, I watched this man of God rise early for prayer. I also saw him rise above his suffering health so he could minister to others. Saji pours out his life, opening the door for many to go and minister to the hungry people of his homeland. Going to South Asia is like fishing for golden trout high in the Wind River Mountains of Wyoming. The Indian people are hungry for Jesus. It's a thrilling place to be a fisher of men.

In Matthew 9:37-38, Jesus says, *"The harvest is plentiful, but the workers are few. Therefore, beseech the Lord of the harvest to send out workers into His harvest."* One afternoon, my interpreter, Andrew Pedron, took me to Dhaba, a village near Nagpur. The people there are very resistant to the Gospel. We held a service in a home, as we did so many other times.

> **The Indian people are hungry for Jesus. It's a thrilling place to be a fisher of men.**

People gathered and five came to receive Christ as personal Savior—a salesman passing by, two local moms, and two young teenage boys. Another afternoon, I asked to play cricket with about thirty players near the Mission India office in Nagpur. After the game, I asked the men if I could preach. They stayed and listened—so hungry. Fifteen of them prayed to receive the Lord. Some of them then came to Pastor Andrew Pedron's home to learn how to grow in their faith.

Later, we visited a village where Christians had previously been martyred for Jesus. Saji knew of my desire to witness, but warned me about this village. I asked him to pray. Later, when Saji was taking a nap, Tendi (one of my interpreters), Vijay (a godly team member), and I went out into the street. Within blocks, many men seemingly had come out of nowhere. They almost surrounded us as we walked.

Vijay said, "I'm going back to the house." Tendi asked me if I sensed anything. I told him it was hostile and I knew it. I asked him if he also wanted to go back to the house. He said, "I only want to know what you are sensing in the Spirit." I told him I could feel the oppression and hostility. Still, knowing I would probably never return to this village, I told him I wanted to preach. I couldn't preach in Hindi, so he was my only hope. He said, "I'm ready!" I counted twenty-six men surrounding us. I said, "I want to preach to you about Jesus." It was like turning on a light in south Florida where cockroaches are abundant. For an instant, you can see the whole tribe of "Amalekites." Then, when the light hits them, they're gone! When I said "Jesus," the crowd of men instantly thinned down to six. I preached the Gospel of Jesus to these eager hearts. It was such an anointing experience to be in sync with my two native brothers, Tendi and Vijay. They anticipated my words. They used the same animations I used. Someday, I will see those six men who remained in Glory. As I preached in the middle of the street, they prayed to receive Jesus into their hearts and lives.

Another incident that affected me deeply took place at the Bible Institute in Nagpur. I was teaching a class of new students just beginning their studies. I wondered if all of them really and truly knew Jesus. It seemed absurd, but the Holy Spirit was leading me to give an invitation to Bible College students. I ended my debate with the Lord, obeyed the Spirit, and gave the invitation. Some of the students started to sob. Ten of them told us that they were not truly saved and then committed their entire lives to the Lord. God is so good. His Word reminds us, *"Be ready in season and out of season"* (2 Timothy 4:2).

One day we walked the perimeter of the land where the seminary in Nagpur now stands. There was nothing there but hope. I knelt with my head on the ground and claimed the land for Jesus—including the adjacent property that was needed for its well. That well now belongs to RIMI. God answers prayer. That day, we also talked to the immigrant workers who lived on the school property. Their homes were made of straw. Despite the abundance of poverty in the land, their dirt floors were kept very clean. I asked the workers if I could preach to them. Fourteen of them listened. One was very resistant, but the other thirteen prayed and gave their lives to the Lord.

One of the most outwardly resistant areas in India is Uttar Pradesh. The most resistant area of the state lies at the foot of the Himalayas in beautiful Nainital. While in Delhi, after our return from Nainital, I was nearly killed by touching my bath water. I had turned off the switch that controlled the coil. However, because wiring in India is not the same as in America, turning the switch off

It was such a joy to see their excitement as God used each of us to become part of His answer to prayer.

was not enough. The coil was still "live." Two-hundred-twenty volts surged through my body! By God's grace I survived, but my left arm tingled for hours.

While in Nainital, we ministered with Saji's brother, David, who works so hard. I was able to see him on the motorcycle the VBS children at our church bought him with their offerings. David organized a family seminar in the Methodist Church right beside Lake Nainital. Fifty-four people gave their lives to Christ at the seminar. Afterwards, the local pastor's wife asked me to come to her home next door. With tears she spoke through an interpreter and said, "I have been praying for you to come here. I didn't know whom I was praying for until you spoke today. Then I knew you were God's answer to my prayer."

Still, my joy was not yet complete in Nainital. Before our arrival, David Lukos had found a house he hoped would become God's answer to their prayers. He and his wife, Bindu, had been praying for a home for themselves and the new Bible Institute in Nainital. The building cost four-thousand rupees. We knelt in a circle and asked God for the money. My home church, Rock Springs Evangelical Free Church in Wyoming, had sent money with me. I had about four thousand rupees left. When we stood, the praying men of God saw the money on the floor. It was such a joy to see their excitement as God used each of us to become part of His answer to prayer.

There are many stories I cannot tell. Here is one final encouraging story. On the way to a village, we passed some Gypsies and I yelled, "Stop!" Saji said we could not stop because we were already late for an appointment. The Spirit was strong in me saying, "We must stop now!" We did. These wandering Gypsies were herding the water buffalo they milk. The five Gypsy men were loud and animated as we approached their tents. One old man, who was smoking a pipe, calmed everyone down. With the help of my interpreter, Tendi, I preached Jesus to them. This old, old man—and four other men—prayed to receive Jesus as the women and children hid in the background and listened. We then gave them follow-up tracts and Bibles. In response, the old man reached into the pocket of his over-the-shoulder trousers. He pulled out an ancient looking tract, worn with use. He explained to us that it had been given to him in Mumbai or Calcutta, I cannot remember, many years before. Someone had been faithful long before we came. Perhaps hundreds of times, this man had read and reread this tract about Jesus and had read it to his people around the evening fires. He told the other men, "God has sent this messenger to explain what I told you was true about knowing Jesus." I believe that entire

Gypsy clan now knows the Lord. Glory! Glory! Glory!

As we made our last trip out to the new Bible Institute at Nagpur, I asked Regi Lukos, who was driving, to pick up a man before he took Saji and me to the airport. In our open jeep, this man prayed with us—bringing the number of those who received Christ during my three weeks in India to 367. I will long remember the blessed joy of this mission trip. God is using Saji, Regi, David, the rest of the Lukos family, and the entire Mission India staff to bring in a harvest of folk to Christ daily. As Vice Chairman of RIMI's Board, I get to hear scores of stories—stories of American pastors and believers going to minister with Saji in South Asia. They come home on fire for Jesus! It is a joy to support Saji and RIMI as a church, a district, and a family. I encourage you to go to South Asia as a fisher of people. They are so hungry for Jesus. *"For the bread of God is that which comes down out of heaven, and gives life to the world.' They said therefore to Him, 'Lord, evermore give us this bread.' Jesus said to them, 'I am the bread of life; he who comes to Me shall not hunger, and he who believes in Me shall never thirst"* (John 6:34-36).

21

INDIA IS MY SECOND HOME

By Laura Grimaldi
Former Director of Development, RIMI

They say, "Home is where the heart is." My heart struggles with the desire to be in two places at once. Certainly, the US is my home. I was born and raised here, and I am proud to be an American. I am proud of America's Christian heritage, and I am proud of what America stands for: freedom! But as much as I love America, I love India, too.

My love for India exists on two levels: social and spiritual. Socially, I see many similarities between the Indian and Italian cultures. I am an Italian-American woman. I was raised in a family of six children. We were poor growing up but never lacked for anything we needed. I had parents who worked very hard to provide for our family, yet they always found time to spend with us kids playing games or helping with our homework. We are a very relational family. Not only were my sisters and brother my best friends, but also EVERYONE was welcome in our home at any time. We couldn't afford to go out to entertain ourselves, so we entertained in our home.

When I go to India, I find that they too are a very friendly, relational people. One day, while I was walking around a neighborhood in India, I passed a man working outside in his gardens. His yard was filled with beautiful plants and flowers. I stopped to compliment him on his yard and ask him the name of a particular plant. Before I could leave I had to go into his home, meet his wife and son and have a glass of coke. They wanted to feed me too, but I had just had lunch. This is something my parents did all of our lives. No one could walk into our house without my mother trying to feed him or her. We learned from them that there are no strangers in the world, only people who had the potential of being our friend. And now, to go half way around the world and experience an acceptance that was a part of my everyday life as a child, and is now missing from the America that I love so much, endeared these people and this country to me.

He used His people in India to touch my heart and change it.

There are other similarities between the Indian and Italian cultures that endeared me to this country. They are family-oriented, they are committed to each other, and they are loyal friends. Older brothers and sisters act like surrogate parents helping to provide for the education and future of younger siblings. All of these things that closely resemble the environment in which I was raised have contributed the sense of "home" I feel in India.

Although the social aspect has influenced my love for India, the spiritual aspect goes much deeper. First of all, for me to enjoy a third world country is a mystery to all who know me. I love my creature comforts, and my idea of camping is the Holiday Inn! I confess that when I joined the staff of RIMI, I did not join because I had a passion for India. I joined for several reasons but that was not one. The first and foremost was because I knew without any doubt that this was where God wanted me, this was the job He had been preparing me for my whole life. The second reason I joined was because it was very evident that God was at work in this ministry and I wanted to be where God was working. And thirdly, I was excited to be working for the Lord full time within the gifting and experience that He had given to me. I never considered the fact that my efforts would be for the advancement of the gospel in a third world country because I knew that my work for this country was in the US. As I made the decision to join, it became apparent that I would need first hand experiences of the work in India in order to be able to share as I traveled, promoting the ministry and developing new partnerships. So, two weeks after I joined RIMI, I went to India for one month. Again, all who knew me couldn't believe that I was going for a month and not just two weeks. It was in the fourth week of my stay in India that something changed in me. My love for India and Her people blossomed. It is now a passion that has grown over the last two and a half years during my tenure with RIMI. It is a God-given passion; there truly is no other explanation. He used His people in India to touch my heart and change it.

The Christians in India are not just lights in the darkness but beacons in the blackest night. They have so little by Western standards and are so happy. They love the Lord with a child-like love, without doubt and with complete trust. It is this love that compels them to sacrifice all for the cause of Christ. There are so many testimonies that I could share with you that would testify to this love and trust. One story is of a pastor in West Bengal. His complete story is too long to share here, but as I was interviewing him he told me a story I want to share with you now.

He had been working in West Bengal for some time and had

developed a network of church planters. He visited these church planters at least once a month. It was time to visit a church planter that lived seventeen miles away, so he and his wife set out early in the morning to walk the seventeen miles to the town where the church planter was ministering. Did you get that? He and his wife walked seventeen miles in one day to go and encourage and help another church planter! They stayed there three days working side by side with the other Christians in that village. No one had room for them in their homes but one man did have a stable and allowed them to sleep there. Sound familiar? They slept in the stable for three nights and then got up early on the fourth day to walk the seventeen miles back home.

As I listened tears came to my eyes, I was ashamed knowing that up until that moment I would not have been willing to sacrifice my comfort for the sake of the gospel—not like that. When he finished this part of the story I thanked him for all the sacrifices that he and his wife have made for Christ; to be willing to sleep in a stable just to minister and encourage. With a smile from ear to ear he responded, "Sacrifice? We rejoiced that we were able to sleep in the same environment that our Lord was born in." It was evident that this experience that closely resembled Christ's experience only brought them closer to Jesus. How could I not love these people? How could I not want to serve side by side with them? What an honor it was for me to be there with him at that moment. His example was so inspirational that I didn't want to go home to the US. I wanted to stay and continue to be influenced by his wonderful sacrificial life.

Yes, my heart struggles with the desire to be in two places at once, here in my beloved United States and in India: my second home.

22

GOD IS MOVING WITH POWER

By Thomas P. Dooley, Ph.D.

Founder of Path Clearer Inc. - Birmingham, Alabama

Jesus said, *"My Father's house shall be a house of prayer for all nations."* Not just for a few, but for *all* nations. His heart is drawn to the nations. *"Ask of Me and I'll give you the nations as an inheritance."* So, when we participate with His will to influence the nations, we are drawn into a journey of maximal impact for the Kingdom of God. Near the top of the list of areas that are experiencing a great move of the Holy Spirit in power today is South Asia.

Asia is on God's heart. It is a fascinating and paradoxical land. The out-pouring of God's desire to bless this particular region is evident in the passionate faces of new believers as they clap feverishly in staccato beat during songs of worship. I have had the privilege to travel within Asia many times as a representative of RIMI's Board of Directors, as well as a friend of Asia. While there I've participated in preaching and teaching in various cities and settings. During these journeys I've visited several regions and have observed firsthand the rapid evangelization of the region with the Gospel of the Jesus Christ.

In 2003, I started declaring publicly that I believed that many Asians would be saved within a decade. This advance would be conditional on the Christian leaders rising up in genuine faith, which could be defined as risk-taking belief in action. This anticipated rapid advance of the Gospel will have a profound effect on the region as the Kingdom of God expands and exerts influence in all aspects of society from education, business, media, arts and culture. Biblical truths and transformed lives will have an ever-increasing impact on the world's largest Hindu population and second largest Muslim community.

At the macro-level millions all across Asia are finding hope. On a more micro-level, consider the following example from one village.

> **This is a time to know that "greater is He that is in you, than he that is in the world."**

One personal highlight of journeying in Asia was a train and auto rickshaw trip taken from Nagpur to Bandara, a village in Central Asia. Saji Lukos and I encouraged approximately twenty people in a small home-based fellowship. The scene provided a stark contrast between the poverty of their living conditions vs. the richness of the joy they have in their faith in Jesus! At dusk literally hundreds of mosquitoes swarmed us in their "living room," coming out of the sewage drain just in front of the doorway to the home where the small group had assembled. We swatted at these buzzing pests in nearly vain attempts to protect our faces and bodies. There were so many mosquitoes that it was impossible to protect oneself from them.

During this brief meeting, we laid hands of prayer on a villager who had been physically persecuted and a young widow woman with three sons. The local elder said that the woman's husband had died as the result of the evil of occult witchcraft. She likely earns only one dollar per day from her manual labors, and the entire responsibility for raising her sons must weigh heavily upon her shoulders. In general widows are not valued highly throughout the two-thirds world. In former days they were even subjected to involuntary sacrifices of their lives upon the death of their husbands. This is no longer the case today, but there is still a measure of devaluing of a widow's life.

In this context it was a privilege to preach briefly to this small audience about the blind beggar who passionately cried out to Jesus in Luke 18. Jesus asked him, *"What do you want from me?"* So, we prayed that God Almighty would grant each of their requests, just as he had for the blind beggar. We asked whether anyone wanted to accept Jesus. Two teenage boys raised their hands confidently and courageously. Two lives were saved in that small home fellowship. The following morning I awoke with tears of compassion and prayer for those who had touched our lives the night before. We received a profound blessing that evening! This type of story is multiplied village by village throughout the region today.

This is a unique time of great potential to reach out to the lost of Asia. This decade shall be unlike any prior decade in all of the history of the nation. In this decade, millions of disciples of the King shall be produced in all nations of Asia from the North, to the South, to the East, and to the West. In this decade, we shall witness the power of the Almighty resting upon this land of great need and opportunity. These results will further demonstrate God's profound power to transform lives and influence an entire region.

In view of these exciting plans of the Almighty Living God for Asia, it shall require voluntary participation by Asia's disciples in spiritual warfare battles. This shall not happen by the hands of lazy men and women. Rather, it shall require hard work and diligence coupled with faith—risk-taking belief in action. This is no time for cowards. This is no time for half-hearted commitment. This is no time for compromise. Rather, this is a time to rise up like Joshua and Caleb to advance the Kingdom of God. This is a time to be strong and courageous. This is a time to be on the offense and not on the defense, merely hanging on. This is a time to know that *"greater is He that is in you, than he that is in the world."*

During the 8th annual RIMI banquet in Chicago, Illinois I encouraged the attendees to *"Get in the boat before it leaves the shore! Get on the train before it leaves the station!"* As God is moving in a new and powerful way in these years, we don't want to miss out on where He is going. Habbakuk 1:5 records, *"Look at the nations and watch – and be utterly amazed. For I am going to do something in your days that you would not believe, even if you were told."* Unparalleled great breakthroughs are happening in the land of Asia. The ministry of RIMI-Mission India is having an increasing role in these changes. The theme that day centered around Hebrews 11:5, *"Without faith it is impossible to please God."* In order to be pleasing to Him we must surrender our own plans and pursue His plans. It is through faith that we'll experience His intended and wonderful risk-taking and rewarding life. Those who live by faith today in Asia will have a profound effect.

God is moving in power throughout all of Asia today. Not only are there many new believers every day, but God remains true to his Word and character revealed in Scripture. He continues to miraculously heal the sick and deliver people influenced by demons. Furthermore, He empowers his disciples with anointed power to perform the callings He has granted as the Holy Spirit has desired. Miraculous healings and manifestations of the demonic realm are common in Asia, and not unlike the accounts described in the New Testament. Perhaps some of this is due to the fact that there is great awareness of the spiritual realm in Asia. By contrast in the Western World, men and women have bought into the Greco-Roman rational lie that humans are merely composed of body and soul (i.e., mind plus emotions) and that we lack a spiritual dimension. But, men have three "compartments" of their identities: body, soul, and spirit. In Asia this reality is easily recognized and embraced. Thus, clear manifestations of the devil's attempted usurping dominion are very common. But, the ultimate victory belongs to Jesus, who has all authority in heaven and on earth. He still delivers and heals today. These manifestations of His power are often seen in ministry in Asia today.

In conclusion, Asia is seeing the power of the Almighty revealed in a most profound season in His divine calendar. There are many being saved, with many being delivered and healed. The power of the Holy Spirit is alive and working in South Asia today.

23

JESUS–ABOVE ALL OTHER GODS

By Linda Kaahanui
Freelance Writer - California

Not South Asia! That, I must confess, was my first thought when I heard Saji Lukos over the phone, calling from Chicago to ask if I would pray about writing a book for RIMI. We had never met. I had never been to South Asia. For that matter, I had never wanted to go to South Asia. This was just one of those things that proves to me that God has a sense of humor and loves to stretch us to places we never thought He would.

As a member of a three-generation family of pastors, I have been to several countries. I have always loved missions and firmly believe that God is all about missions. Didn't Jesus make the ultimate missionary journey when He left heaven and came to this planet? But the thought of India and its culture just did not appeal to me. For some reason, I had the same silly fear that I did before I adopted my first child, "What if I don't bond?"

I spent a month that summer in Mozambique, determined to get an answer from God regarding South Asia before I left. He answered loud and clear – go. So, I packed up all my ignorant expectations, questions and assumptions and went. You've heard of people with baggage? Fortunately, I didn't have to pay for the extra weight.

My dear friend, Jeanne Jasses-Counter, went with me. God used the month of March in 2005 to forever seal India in our hearts. Like the moment I laid eyes on my daughter for the first time, I loved South Asia and her people as soon as I arrived. I realized God was doing something supernatural, all my reservations instantly dropped away, replaced by a compassion for the suffering I saw and a holy anger at the obvious, terrible ravages of the enemy inflicted on the people for so many centuries.

> **The goodness of Jesus is not just a theological concept in South Asia, it is practical reality.**

Jeanne and I were taken to several villages where we lived with local people, slept in their homes, prayed and worshipped with them, sat on the floor and ate with our hands with them, laughed a lot and cried with them. OK, we bonded after all. What was I afraid of? It was wonderful.

Most of all, we listened. (I was supposed to be researching for a book, remember?) During that month, I think I interviewed over 50 people, including Bible School students, pastors, Mission India staff, and Saji's family members. All together, their stories formed a picture of what it means to be a Jesus Follower in South Asia. I don't say "Christian" because that phrase is almost meaningless in some contexts. I'm talking about those who are truly in love with their Lord and are committed to following Him wherever He leads, wherever that is and whatever that costs.

I witnessed a passion for Jesus that humbled me in the profoundest way. As I listened to their stories, some common threads ran through them all. These Jesus Followers know at least three important things:

The goodness of Jesus is not just a theological concept in South Asia, it is practical reality. I don't think I met a single believer who had not come to Jesus because of some supernatural manifestation of God's goodness. All, yes ALL, had experienced healing, demonic deliverance, or some other miraculous event. Jesus is revealing Himself to the people of South Asia. In the midst of unimaginable poverty and suffering, He is showing Himself to be GOOD!

Second, they know Jesus will cost them something – perhaps everything. Saji's own story is just one example. Many tears flowed as believers told of family rejection, village ostracism and ongoing, violent persecution. I met students who could not go home – ever. Some Bible college students were already on the "hit lists" of radical, anti-Christian groups that try to intimidate through beatings and even murder. Yet, through the tears, a joy radiated that only shines in those who know "the fellowship of his suffering."

Third, they understand their calling. Maybe that's what is missing in so many Western churches. We have no idea why we're still here. We're just killing time until the Rapture. That kind of aimless, purposeless Christianity breeds the complacency, apathy and boredom that runs rampant in our religious circles. We are not about our Father's business because we are not intimate with Him enough to understand His business. He is passionate about bringing His lost children home! We are called to be imitators of Christ, the One who came to seek and to save. We are called to announce the Kingdom of God and usher in the life of that Kingdom to a dying world. We are called to invade and reclaim the enemy-occupied territory of this world. Believe me, South

Asia has been occupied, stomped, mauled and decimated by the enemy long enough! The Jesus Followers of South Asia today are answering the call to say, "Enough! The Kingdom is at hand!"

I watched the graduates from Mission India's Theological Seminary and Bible Training Centers. I have never seen such zealous energy for the Gospel just waiting to be unleashed. I could not help but think of racehorses held behind the starting gate. They want to go! To run the race set before them! Many students had already used their school breaks to go as pastors to un-reached villages, planting churches in places where no one had heard the name of

May we be as surrendered and obedient in our calling to send as they are in their calling to go.

Jesus before. It amazed me that some of these students had not even accepted Christ as their Savior until *after* coming to Bible college, yet these "baby" Christians were already healing the sick, casting out demons, and populating Heaven! They know He is good. He is worth everything. He has called them to the harvest fields.

I wonder if we, in the West, have learned so well. We have a doctrinal understanding that God is good, but it's clear by our priorities that we think other stuff is better. Thinking we are rich, we have become so poor! May God, who is rich in mercy, grant us a fuller revelation of His extravagant goodness! Enough so, that we are ruined for anything less than Him alone.

We have little understanding of counting the cost. We live no different than our unsaved neighbors. We think we can have the world and Jesus too! Therefore, we have missed out on much of life in the Kingdom realm because, like the rich man in Jesus' illustration, we want to hang on to stuff that just won't pass through the eye of God's needle. Whatever the cost, may we learn from our brothers and sisters in South Asia, the "surpassing greatness of knowing Christ Jesus my Lord..."

May we join them in answering the call of our Lord. Maybe we can't personally head off into some remote village, but we can be just as vitally involved. We have one Father, and all of us children are to be about His business. When we pray earnestly, He can enable us to give or to go or to send. The great news is that God equally rewards the go-er and the sender! RIMI (Mission India) has trained up hundreds of young men and women who are prepared to fulfill God's calling on their lives. The harvest is ripe. The Good News of the Kingdom is on their lips and in their hearts. They are ready to go. Some of us are called to send them. May we be as surrendered and obedient in our calling to send as they are in their calling to go.

God has changed my initial "Not India!" to "Yes, India!" I love what I see Jesus doing there. He is revealing Himself to be who He is, the Light of the World who shines even in the darkest, most desperate places. He is Jesus.

24

NUMBERS
FROM THE 10/40 WINDOW

By Douglas Steward
Businessman - Michigan

South Asia – The Challenge

My prayers for the redemption of the people of South Asia actually began many years before my involvement with RIMI. I was a college student, fresh in my faith in Jesus Christ, and eager to see great continents and countries won for Christ. A friend of mine had mentioned South Asia as a destination that particularly needed our prayers. He explained to me that India had a population that, at the time, was approaching 1 billion people, many of whom were largely un-evangelized.

Even more daunting was the fact that South Asia contains more than 4,000 different *people groups*. People groups can be defined as the classifying of people by religion, culture, language or geography. South Asia has a complex social structure. The caste system of South Asia comes from the custom of marrying only within the limits of a clan or tribe. The word "caste" is derived from the Portuguese word "caste" which means a breed or race. The caste system established Brahmin control over the majority. It pervades all religious and social structures in South Asia. Caste discrimination is forbidden by the national constitution, but is socially important for the vast majority of the population. There are an estimated 6,400 castes in India alone. Each is its own people group because of the social barriers that separate them. Jesus told his disciples that repentance and forgiveness of sins will be preached to *all nations* (Luke 24:47). Believers representing every nation, tribe, people and language will appear before the Lord and His throne in heaven (Revelation 7:9).

All South Asian people groups will be represented before the throne of God. I decided right then, while a new believer in college, to begin praying for an opportunity to take part in bringing the gospel to South Asia. For many years, I was not sure how I was to accomplish this.

Meeting Saji Lukos

When I first heard Saji speak at my church, I was stunned by his sense of purpose; his *strategy* to reach *all* of South Asia. He was truly concerned that thousands of people die in South Asia every day without knowing Christ! Saji understood that man's main purpose is to glorify God by knowing Him and by making Him known (the Great Commission). This is what I had been praying for all these years!

Saji had plans to send out at least 1,000 indigenous church planters every year and plant 100,000 house churches during his lifetime. His 20 year goals were for 100 million people to hear about Christ and 10 million to make new decisions for Christ. He was in the process of constructing church buildings in strategic areas in every South Asian state. RIMI was leading 100 evangelistic meetings every year.

Paul the Apostle told the Romans that he had fully preached the gospel from Jerusalem to Illyricum (Romans 15:19), a total land mass of over three hundred thousand square miles! He accomplished this by establishing churches in strategic cities and regions. Saji Lukos is planting churches in strategic cities and regions with the same goal in mind—to see the gospel preached to all residents of South Asia.

The 10/40 Window

In the west, the gospel is available almost everywhere. There are churches in every community, to the extent that there seems to be more churches than available church members. Christian radio and television permeate the airwaves. Evangelistic programs through church and para-church organizations are implemented every year. There is not a person I have met in the West who has not heard, usually more than once, of the message of salvation. If a person seeks God in the West, he or she can find Him with ease. This is not so in many other areas of the world. There is a region of un-reached people of our world who live in a rectangular-shaped window. The window extends from West Africa to East Asia, from ten degrees north to forty degrees north of the equator. This area, known as the 10/40 Window, is laden with Muslims, Hindus, and Buddhists, but few Christians. It is home to the majority of the world's un-evangelized people. These people have minimal or no knowledge of the gospel, and no opportunity to respond to it. South Asia is located within the 10/40 Window.

"How then will they call on Him in whom they have not believed? How will they believe in Him whom they have not heard? And how will they hear without a preacher?" (Romans 10:14)

The 10/40 Window is only one-third of earth's total land area, but nearly two-thirds of the world's people reside in it. That's 4 billion people living in 59 countries where the majority of their land mass is in the 10/40 Window.

Of the 50 least evangelized countries in the world, 37 are within *the 10/40 Window.* Yet those 37 countries comprise 97% of the total population of the 50 least evangelized countries! In other words, the vast majority of people who have no contact with the gospel live in this area. Other religions hostile to Christianity thrive in this region. It is estimated that 2.7 billion Hindus, Buddhists, and Muslims live in the 10/40 Window.

The poorest populations live in the 10/40 Window. More than 8 out of 10 of the poorest people live in this region of the world. On average, they exist on less than $500 per person per year. 2.4 billion people (almost 40% of the world's population) live on less then $1.40 per day in the 10/40 Window. And yet, only 8% of all pastors work among them.

Students at RIMI

From time to time, I am invited to teach at the Mission India Theological Seminary. I have had the opportunity to meet many young South Asian nationals from all geographical regions of South Asia and several different people groups. They are at the Seminary to get their degrees and be trained to become the next generation of pastors, church-planters, and evangelists for South Asia. Their energy for God and His Word, for His purposes stirs my soul. They are the future of South Asia. They will carry the gospel to many who have never heard of the Man who died on the cross.

Most of the students come from humble backgrounds, and Mission

India is the best place they have ever stayed. They are united in dreams of serving the Lord in spreading His gospel. They do not worry about the luxuries of life, as young people do in Western countries. They have nothing more than the clothes and bedding given them at the seminary.

These students, when they are prepared to enter the field, will have little support from their countrymen. It must come from places like America, where our resources are great. The $60 a month in support these budding church planters and evangelists will need is very little of our disposable income. Compare this to the cost of sending Western workers to South Asia.

Indigenous Workers

The best way to reach South Asia is through training and sending their own national people. They are already on the field. Indigenous workers can evangelize entire villages, plant new churches, build medical clinics, schools, and childcare centers. They know the language and the customs, which is particularly important in a diverse culture like South Asia. Each district in South Asia is essentially its own people group with its own language and culture.

A national church planter is a South Asian citizen; they have all the rights to stay and minister for as long as they like. The indigenous church planter cannot be expelled when there is political unrest. This is important with the rising tide of nationalism in the world. Government officials look with disfavor upon foreign missions. They believe it to be an invasion of their culture.

CHAPTER TWENTY FOUR

Piercing the Darkness

Paul said his commission was to preach the gospel to the Gentiles in order *"to open their eyes so that they may turn from darkness to light and from the dominion of Satan to God"* (Acts 16:18). Jesus said, *"I have come as Light into the world, so that everyone who believes in Me will not remain in darkness"* (John 12:46).

"Darkness and light" are metaphors for the blinding effects of the sin-ravaged world and the message of the Gospel that penetrates this darkness. The people of God are called to manifest His truth and light to the rest of the world.

"You are the light of the world. A city set on a hill cannot be hidden; nor does anyone light a lamp and put it under a basket, but on the lamp stand, and it gives light to all who are in the house. "Let your light shine before men in such a way that they may see your good works, and glorify your Father who is in heaven." (Matthew 5:14-16).

South Asia resides in darkness. The opportunities for people across Asia to hear the Gospel are few, and may be non-existent in many areas. Yet, through RIMI I am able to participate in "shedding the darkness" by the financial and prayer support I give. This is why I invest strategically in South Asia. I want to participate in the Gospel's penetration of the darkness. I want to use the resources I have to their fullest. I want to be part of the Great Commission.

A Remarkable Family

Saji, by the power of God, is surrounded by a remarkable family. Each of the Lukos family, including his father and mother, now share new life in Christ, and serve the Lord with fervor and faith.

Moni is very good for Saji. Their hearts share the call to RIMI's ministry together. She is a wise counselor and helpmate and a significant part of God's blessing to Saji and the ministries of RIMI and Mission India. Maryann is also a blessing to them both. Both love to accompany Saji to India and encourage the leaders and Mercy Home children.

Saji's brother, Regi, is a powerful Mission India leader. He is also an exceptional builder. He has overseen the construction of all the Mission India facilities in India. Through his use of God-given skills and capabilities, he has helped develop many well-used and effective facilities. These are invaluable resources for the ministries' effectiveness. He maximizes the expenditure of every rupee wisely. Regi's

> **Darkness and light are metaphors for the blinding effects of the sin-ravaged world and the message of the gospel that penetrates this darkness. The people of God are called to manifest His truth and light to the rest of the world.**

contribution to the MITS Campus and churches around India are vital.

I was privileged to participate in the wedding of Saji's sister, Jessy. It was held in Kerala, India—Saji's home state. At the wedding I observed again Lukos' family love for Christ and witness to India. They are a testimony to the saving and keeping power of God!

It is also a powerful testimony to see how Saji has faithfully fulfilled his role as eldest son and spiritual head of the family to his siblings. In this way he demonstrates the sufficiency of Christ for all to see. All his siblings, Lissy, Sunny, Regi, Matthews, David, Jessy, and Ancy have come through spiritual darkness to the light of the Gospel. Each one is ministering in different ways alongside Saji to advance the Gospel in India. Saji Lukos is indeed a part of a most spiritually remarkable family.

For India

Our great God is working mightily through RIMI and Mission India to make a significant impact on India. God is continuing to faithfully empower Saji to be His instrument for mobilizing the church to reach India and the world for Christ. God willing, we have only seen the beginnings of an increasingly extensive and powerful work of God through RIMI. Trials and sufferings only strengthen the zeal, faith and perseverance of the ministry and its leaders. May God give Saji India—and all Indians worldwide! Saji is a global leader with a global vision!

"Therefore, since we have so great a cloud of witnesses surrounding us, let us also lay aside every encumbrance and the sin which so easily entangles us, and let us run with endurance the race that is set before us." Hebrews 12:1 (NASB)

25

THE JOY
OF STRATEGIC INVESTING

By Bob Ancha
Chairman, Pinnacle Forum - Prescot, Arizona

E ven though I had been to a RIMI banquet in the Chicago area in
the fall of 1998, it was not until January 11, 2000 that my wife and
I met Saji Lukos on a personal basis here in Prescott, Arizona. Without
applying any pressure, Saji explained his vision for reaching the 1.2
billion people in South Asia through RIMI. That vision included the
plans for the Nagpur campus developed by Bob Schill. Both Saji and
Bob Schill drove up to Prescott from Phoenix on March 24, 2001, and
shared with us their master plan for the 30 acre complex. They asked
us to pray about sponsoring the very first girls' dormitory for twenty-
four young women. We did prayerfully consider it, and the Lord led us
to fund the construction of what turned out to be the Ancha Hostel
which I dedicated on April 6, 2002. It was such a joy to see the young
ladies in their rooms and the flower garden that they planted and
maintained at the back of the building.

It was my pleasure on that day to be one of the keynote speakers
at the graduation ceremony where I challenged the graduates to preach

the Word using 2 Timothy 4:2 and 5, *"Be ready in season and out of season. Convince, rebuke, exhort, with all longsuffering, but you be watchful in all things, endure afflictions, do the work of an evangelist, fulfill your ministry."*

During the next day, Sunday April 7, 2002 I was able to preach through a translator at the Mission India church in Nagpur using as my text Romans 6:6, *"Knowing this, that our old man was crucified with HIM, that the body of sin might be done away with, that we should no longer be slaves of sin."* God blessed the message and saw fit at the end of the service to have several men raise their hands, indicating a desire to receive Christ as Lord and Savior.

Why Not Support National Pastors?

For many years I have been burdened with the fact that it costs so much to send a Western pastor overseas because they may take up to two years to learn the language and culture of that country. At RIMI's Nagpur campus in India, church planters with a Bible Theology degree can be trained in less than a year and sent out to some of the remote cities and villages for approximately $1,000 to $2,000 per year (depending upon whether single or with a family). Most importantly, national church planters already know the language and culture of the people. That is a huge difference from the $50,000 to $75,000 it takes to send Western church planters who do not know the language and aren't familiar with the culture. There is a role for Western church planters, but if we are to reach the 1.2 billion people of India, we need to look at the cost-effectiveness. Perhaps, sending 50 national church planters out rather than one Western worker to do the same work is the way to accomplish this.

I like what Tom Telford has written in his landmark book on

missions entitled, *Today's All Star Mission Churches*. He quotes Dr. David Nicholas, Senior Pastor of the Spanish River Church in Boca Raton, Florida, who stated, "It would be just fine with me if Spanish River Church never sent another Western worker overseas! In fact, we'll probably never support another traditional worker again." It is equally thrilling to hear the story described in his book starting on page fifteen concerning Dr. John Piper's Bethlehem Baptist Church in Minneapolis, Minnesota. As they came under the influence of ACMC (Advancing Churches in Mission Commitment), Mission Pastor Tom Steller reports that fourteen convictions came out of a study which are now driving missions at Bethlehem.

Conviction number eight states, "They have come to see that the unique task of missions, as opposed to evangelism, is to plant the church among people groups where it does not exist. When the church has been planted in all the people groups of the earth, and the elect have been gathered in from all the 'tongues and tribes and nations,' then the great commission will be complete. The task of missions is planting the church among all the peoples, not necessarily winning all the people."

> **There is a role for Western church planters, but if we are to reach the 1.2 billion people of India, we need to look at the cost-effectiveness. Perhaps, sending 50 national church planters out rather than one Western worker to do the same work is the way to accomplish this.**

Conviction number nine goes on to say, "The need of the hour is for thousands of new Paul-type workers, a fact which is sometimes obscured by the quantity of Timothy-type workers...not that we diminish the sacrifice and preciousness of Timothy-type workers, but we realize what the utterly critical, uniquely missionary need is in the world, namely, there are thousands of people groups with no access to the saving knowledge of Jesus. Only Paul-type workers can reach them. That must be a huge priority for us. Without the Gospel everything is in vain."

Why not be Generous?

So many Christians feel that if they tithe 10% to their local church and give a little extra to a few missionary organizations, their obligation for Kingdom work is met. A book that all truly generous Christians should read, and ask the Holy Spirit what he would like them to do as a lasting legacy after they are called home to Glory, is the book, *The Eternity Portfolio* by Alan Gotthardt. In chapter four, Alan provides a formula for exponential generosity which warrants a ten percent giving amount with increasing percentages on the remaining income. The author goes on to say,

"… a proactive strategy is the best way to position yourself according to this passage in the Psalms: 'if riches increase, do not set your heart on them' (Psalm 62:10). There is a tremendous freedom that comes from knowing you are going to give away a larger and larger piece of that next dollar. You have not set your heart upon it, so whether or not God will bring more wealth your way does not concern you anymore."

Some of us who are older and have reached retirement age have realized that some of our most productive years are still ahead of us when we stop making a living and start making a life by contributing to the welfare of the poor and downtrodden. If we really think about it, God's plan for us to reach the world might be broken down into three basic components as outlined in Chapter Six of Alan Gotthardt's book:

1. Evangelism (reaching people with the Gospel of Christ)

2. Discipleship (teaching Christians Biblical truths about how to live as a disciple of Christ)

3. Mercy (ministering to physical, emotional, and spiritual needs in the name of Christ)

An investment with RIMI enables us as contributors to fulfill all three areas so close to the heart of God. RIMI has over 1200 church planters and 4,000 house churches winning and discipling perhaps 20,000 people to Christ each year. In addition, 22 Mercy Homes throughout India minister to and take care of orphaned and disadvantaged children. We know of no more cost-effective ministry anywhere in the United States that does all three ministries as effectively as RIMI.

That's why my wife and I continue to invest in RIMI. We have provided funds for a Prayer Tower in the center of Nagpur campus, where several students pray twenty-four hours a day. We also provided funds for

Our giving to RIMI has provided a sense of fulfillment and joy that is unspeakable.

an important bridge on the campus to the dairy farm that my good friend, Norm Anderson from Chicago, provided funds for. It was my privilege to return to the Nagpur Campus in March 2003 and dedicate these buildings.

Again, in 2004, our hearts turned towards the third component of the important triangle discussed above: Evangelism, Discipleship, and Mercy. We next funded a Mercy Home for fifty girls, named for my daughter, Cheri Sommerville, who has displayed a real Christ-like attitude to her two adopted children.

This Mercy Home will not only house fifty girls, but includes a care building with a living/dinning area, community area, two bedrooms, two guest rooms, infirmary, kitchen, laundry, nursery, five bathrooms, and storage rooms.

All six of our Prescott family members returned to India in March 2006, as we dedicated the building to the glory of God. Our seventeen-year-old granddaughter, Becky Sommerville gave a Bible study to the girls present and brought gifts for each one of them. Our giving to RIMI has provided a sense of fulfillment and joy that is unspeakable.

26

Partnership Opportunities

Dear Brothers and Sisters,

The time is *now* to answer God's call to reach out to the many people dying every day without knowing Jesus Christ. We cannot waste time. Today, I urge you to partner with us in bringing the Gospel of hope to those untold millions who need to hear it. Listed in the back of this book are ways that you can partner with us to reach the lost. Your small gift, my friend, can go a long way in furthering the Kingdom of God.

Will you partner with us?

Sponsor a Native Church Planter

RIMI now has 1,200 church planters out in the field, but many more are needed. Our goal is to send out thousands of church planters into the harvest field. Every year 600-1000 students graduate from our Seminary and our regional Bible schools. Presently, many graduates are waiting for sponsorships. It takes between $90-$180 to fully sponsor a national missionary depending upon family size and location. This includes family and ministry expenses. You can help support a national missionary for as little as $30 per month. When you sponsor, you will receive a testimony and photo of your missionary and our monthly newsletter.

One Church Can Make a Difference

Intentional Strategic Partnerships

RIMI is looking for churches or groups who will make a long-term commitment to adopt a region or a people group for saturation evangelism and church planting. You can adopt a district of ten counties—with a population of 2-3 million unreached people—for around $1200 per month. Through your sponsorship your local church participates in planting hundreds of new churches in South Asia. This creates new excitement and passion for the lost at home resulting in the growth of your own church family. Your partnership will be facilitated under the supervision of a national district leader. An annual update of the ministry you partner with will be sent. Your church or group is encouraged to send short-term missions teams to teach or assist in various ministry projects.

Sponsor a Child Today

Our goal is to reach 25,000 children during the next twenty years. There are currently hundreds of children waiting for support. Some of these children come from families who are so poor they cannot provide daily food for their households. Others are orphans who have no family to care for them. You can sponsor a child for only $30 per month. This provides food, shelter, and clothing. Each child will also receive Biblical training and hear of the love of Christ. When you sponsor a child, you will receive a biography and photo of your child and our monthly newsletter.

Sponsor a Church Hall

Our goal is to build 3,000 church halls. Once a missionary has a good number of people regularly attending the weekly service, they often find themselves in need of a church building. The building provides protection from the elements as well as some security from the local persecution. Each building is capable of holding 100-150 people. There is also an attached parsonage for the missionary to live in. The church hall is used 24/7 for various ministry activities. A typical church building with the parsonage costs around $10,000.

Sponsor a Bible Training Center

RIMI's goal is to establish at least one Bible Training Center in every state of India. Presently we have Bible training centers in 23 of the 28 Indian states. We also have the Mission India Theological Seminary in Nagpur, central India. It costs $2500 per month to sponsor a Bible training center for 25 students.

Ministry Tools

Tracts

Just as they are here in America, tracts can be a very important tool for reaching people in India. It is something that people can take with them and read in their own time. They can be easily transported and passed from person to person. Tracts are $1 per packet.

Bibles

Our goal is to buy and distribute 50,000 Bibles in South Asia each year. Our desire is to give a Bible to every new believer and to anyone seriously interested in learning about Christ. A Bible is an essential tool. Though plentiful here, they are rare in Indian homes. We can distribute Bibles in the native languages of India for only $2 each.

Dhari

It is common in India to sit on the floor or ground for meetings. During the winter, the floors are cold. The Dhari is a floor rug that can cover a 10' x 10' area. This provides warmth and cushioning as well as helping to keep people's garments clean. A typical Dhari costs $50.

Gas Light

In many areas where our missionaries live and visit, electricity is unreliable or even unavailable. A lantern can provide enough light to enable safe travel during the nighttime hours and for conducting evening meetings. As most people are day laborers, they often will not have time to listen or attend a meeting unless it is at night. A lantern allows the missionary to have some light for these meetings. Each lantern costs $50.

Bicycle

A bicycle enables a missionary to reach more villages and visit more people than they can by foot. The villages that our missionaries minister in are usually spread out with few roads between them. By foot, a missionary can reach only a few villages a day. With a bicycle, 2-3 times as many villages can be reached. We can provide a good quality bicycle for a missionary for $100.

Gas Stove

Many of our missionaries live in rented rooms owned by local people. Cooking facilities are not provided. In most villages gas connections are not available and wood is expensive. We can provide a propane stove for cooking for $100.

Motorbike

Mission India area coordinators visit each missionary serving in their district at least once a month to encourage and mentor them. RIMI's goal is to provide each area coordinator with a motorbike to facilitate their travel. Each motorbike costs $1,000.

Invite a RIMI Speaker

The harvest is ripe in South Asia. We must not miss this opportunity to reap the souls God has prepared. By inviting a RIMI speaker to your church or group, you can hear firsthand about the mighty work God is doing in India and beyond. Many of our workers are persecuted by their own families and those who hate the spread of Christianity. Every day people are being delivered from demonic oppression, healed from various diseases, and freed from the power of sin. As you hear these stories of transformation, you will be refreshed, inspired and encouraged!

Ministry Opportunities

Short-term Missions

RIMI provides short-term opportunities to strategically be involved in assisting national workers. Short-term opportunities include teaching in our seminary and Bible schools, serving in our Mercy Homes, serving in our hospital and medical camps, translations projects, and a variety of other ministries. If interested, please call the RIMI office at 847-265-0630 or email us at ministry@rimi.org.

Long-term Missions

RIMI provides long-term missions opportunities for qualified individuals to serve among the unreached people groups in South Asia, Africa, Middle East, and Europe. If interested, please call the RIMI office at 847-265-0630 or email us at ministry@rimi.org.

North American Ministry Opportunities

God is bringing thousands of people from darkness to light in South Asia. You can be part of this great harvest. Planting churches, training leaders, and serving poor and needy children cannot be done without RIMI's home staff. Each person on our staff is called by God to minister behind the scenes in support of our national workers and their global partners in the West. If you hunger to impact eternity, RIMI is waiting for you. Ministry opportunities currently available include:

- Managers/Regional Coordinators
- Administrative Support
- Receptionist
- Data Entry

- Grant Writers

- Graphic Designers

- Event Coordinators

- Book Keeper

- Short/Long-term Missions Coordinator

- Script/Book Writers

- Telephone Specialist

- Web Developer

- Media Coordinator (Video/Photo)

REV. SAJI LUKOS (a graduate of Trinity International University, Deerfield, IL) is founder and president of Reaching Indians Ministries International (RIMI) in USA and Mission India (MI) in India. God is using these ministries to reach South Asians with the good news of Christ worldwide. Saji has written numerous missions related articles and a book published in India, entitled, Heroes of the Cross. He has traveled to many countries and led thousands into God's Kingdom. His single-minded passion is to raise up 100,000 Christ-like, global leaders to fulfill RIMI's God-given vision. Saji lives near Chicago, Illinois, with his wife, Moni and daughter Maryann.

For more information about RIMI
(and to find out about other materials available)
please visit

www.rimi.org

You can also contact us at:

RIMI
P.O. Box 688
Round Lake Beach, IL 60073, USA
847-265-0630
info@rimi.org

Transformed For A Purpose

REPLY CARD

I would like to help the ministry by sponsoring:
❑ Child $30   ❑ Missionary: ❑$30   ❑$60   ❑$120
❑ Bicycle $100   ❑ Motorbike $1,000   ❑ Where Most Needed $_____

Please send me ___ more books at $24.95 + $4.50 S/H each for a total of
$_____ (call for multiple shipping rates)

Total Funds Enclosed $_____

_____
[NAME]

_____
[ADDRESS]

_____
[ADDRESS]

_____
[CITY/STATE/ZIP]

_____
[PHONE]

_____
[PRAISES AND PRAYERS]

_____
[EMAIL]

CREDIT CARD TYPE: ❑Visa   ❑Master Card   ❑American Express   ❑Discover

_____
[NAME AS IT APPEARS ON THE CARD]

_____ ____/____ $_____
[NUMBER]   [EXPIRATION DATE]   [AMOUNT]

_____
[SIGNATURE]

Make checks payable to RIMI

RIMI
PO Box 688, Round Lake Beach, IL 60073
Phone:(847) 265-0630   **Fax:** (847) 265-0642
Email:SLukos@RIMI.org   **Web:** www.RIMI.org

RIMI is a 501(c)(3) organization and all donations, except for books, are tax deductible. A receipt will be sent for those items that qualify.